Quiet Moments

FOR PARENTS & OTHER CAREGIVERS

Devotions of Comfort and
Encouragement for Stressful Times

MARY VAUGHN ARMSTRONG

LIFEJOURNEY
BOOKS

LifeJourney Books™ is an imprint of Chariot Family Publishing
a division of David C. Cook Publishing Co.
David C. Cook Publishing Co., Elgin, Illinois 60120
David C. Cook Publishing Co., Weston, Ontario
Nova Distribution Ltd., Newton Abbot, England

QUIET MOMENTS FOR PARENTS
AND OTHER CAREGIVERS
©1992 by Mary Vaughn Armstrong

Cover design by Koechel/Peterson & Associates
First Printing, 1992
Printed in the United States of America
96 95 94 93 92 5 4 3 2 1

CIP applied for
ISBN 1-55513-664-8

For our beloved children:
Ann, Lee and Leslie,
John and Rita, Matt and Lori

But they who wait for the Lord shall renew their strength, they shall mount up with wings like eagles, they shall run and not be weary, they shall walk and not faint.

Isaiah 40:31

Out from under the clouds

∽

READ MATTHEW 7:24-29.
"And the rain descended, and the floods came, and the winds blew, and burst against that house; and yet it did not fall, for it had been founded upon the rock." Matthew 7:25

We've got to get out of this climate," a friend groaned. "It rains over half the year—it's getting to my wife, and I know it's getting to me."

Recent studies demonstrate a clear link between the absence of light and clinical depression. People living in cloudy, drizzly, or overcast areas, where weeks may pass between glimpses of the sun, often experience deep discouragement. When light is restored, real or artificial, they feel happier and far more energetic.

Day in, day out responsibility for another person can be like living under a weeping cloud. Without realizing it, many who carry that load sink into a grey mindset that whispers, "Things are all right today, but watch out! Tomorrow there's going to be a storm." Depression is all too common among parents and caregivers of every age.

Today's Bible reading tells how you can shine light on your darkest days. As you make time to *listen* to Jesus and to *act* upon His words, you will be like the wise man in the parable. Depression may threaten like distant thunder, but it will not come near you. Day or night, in sunlight or downpour, you and yours will stand upon solid rock.

PRAYER: Thank You, Lord, that You alone are my anchor through every storm. When I feel most discouraged, help me to remember that I will not slip, for You have bound me to Yourself.

Words that will harm,
words that will heal

READ *II TIMOTHY 1:1-4.*

"...To Timothy, my beloved son: Grace, mercy and peace from God the Father and Christ Jesus our Lord." II Timothy 1:2

"Mom, hurry! John fell off his bike and hurt his leg!"

Matt's words swept through the kitchen window, their urgency unmistakable. I punched off the stove burners and ran outside. At the edge of the porch nine-year-old John rocked back and forth, clutching one leg.

"My bike hit a rock and I slid on the dirt. It hurts so much." Tears filled his eyes. "Do we have something that'll take the sting out, Mom?"

We did, and fifteen minutes later John was outside again, the angry abrasion covered with soothing ointment and a non-stick bandage.

Maybe you haven't fallen off a bike, but the sting of a family member's hateful words to you is every bit as painful. Or perhaps, in a moment of impatience and hurry, you've said cruel things to a loved one. And now you'd give anything to take those words back.

In today's scripture Paul refers to Timothy as "beloved," a term more soothing to its recipient than any ointment. Paul's example provides an antidote for things once said and now regretted—the transforming, two-way power of a gentle word.

Take a minute right where you are to think of five words that especially touch your own heart. Now say them out loud, the way you'd like to hear them spoken to you.

PRAYER: Forgive me, Lord, for inflicting pain by the things I say. Please infuse every word I speak today with Your soothing love.

So much to do, so little time

⸎

READ PSALM 57:7-11.
"My heart is steadfast, O God, my heart is steadfast." Psalm 57:7

I jerked open the car door, slung my purse strap over one shoulder, stole a glance at my watch for the second time in as many minutes, and dashed into the market. I'd be later than I promised the baby sitter, but only by a few minutes if I rushed.

The store's endless musak wrapped its plastic sound around my ears as I wrestled a shopping cart from the stack and whirled toward the tuna aisle. I threw eight cans into my basket, careened around the corner, and crashed headlong into another cart.

Startled and obviously frightened, the young mother at its handle end pulled back as she slipped one arm protectively around the baby propped in the carrier. I apologized several times, circled far to the right, and picked up milk and margarine at a subdued and chastened pace. What if I'd hit her leg, or her hand . . . or her baby? Constantly taking care of someone else makes careless racers of us all. Time, our scarcest commodity, oozes too easily through our fingers, and we rush to stanch the hemorrhage.

The unhurried Christ models God's master pattern of a quiet spirit. With fleeting time to complete His ministry, He walked through the hours of each day focused on the moment. As in today's psalm, His heart was fixed and steadfast as He trusted in the Father's timing. The result? For Him, as for us, completion of all the Father asked, one day at a time.

PRAYER: O Father, forgive my feverish pace, especially during (add your own words). Brand into my mind the example of Your unhurried Son.

Facing ingratitude with the right attitude

———— ∽ ————

READ I THESSALONIANS 5:14-18.
"And we urge you, brethren . . . be patient with all men." I Thessalonians 5:14

I can't believe your mother's ninety-four! I enjoyed talking to her in the restaurant today —she's delightful."

"When she's away from the retirement complex, she is."

"What about when she's there?"

"She won't talk to anyone. She's furious at having to live in group housing. She's never accepted having to move out of her own house—even though the doctor said she wasn't safe there." My friend laughed slightly. "She's only nice to me because I'm her lifeline to the outside world!"

Is there someone like that in your life right

now? Across town or maybe under the same roof? By word and action, does a family member deny the reality of his or her present situation? Are you barely tolerated, the frequent target of thinly veiled criticism? Right now, name that person before the Lord.

In today's letter to the Thessalonians Paul gives instruction applicable to the most thankless caregiving. His verbs are active and powerful: we are told to admonish, encourage, and help. We are to be patient with everyone, aiming always to show kindness and do good.

A ninety-four year old woman who refuses to talk is angry at two things: her situation and her age. Her daughter's task is to admonish if needed, to encourage, and to help. The mother's task is to come to grips with the realities of her long life, something no one else can do for her.

PRAYER: Father, help me to stop trying to make everyone happy, especially (repeat the name of the one you identified earlier). Teach me to recognize behavior that You alone can change.

Prepared for the battle

———————— ∞ ————————

READ ECCLESIASTES 3:1-11A.
"He has made everything beautiful in its time."
Ecclesiastes 3:11a

"Time out!"

How many of us remember spending hours—even days—cheering at a softball, baseball, or football game? Every so often, as by the click of an invisible stopwatch, the umpire or referee would stop play while team members huddled, made plans, and regrouped.

But in life there often seems to be no time out—no period for refreshing, preparation, or strategy. A year after his divorce a single father finds himself raising a daughter he barely knows. He longs for time to shift gears, but there is none.

Though this uneasy parent doesn't realize it, God has amply prepared him already. He has provided a two-bedroom house, a degree in social work, wonderful neighbors, and for both of them, the desire to try. In His economy this father and daughter need no time out. They are ready.

The Lord blends each of our varied experiences, backlights them with His love, and from them shapes new seasons in our lives. Some are short, others seem to last forever. But in the end He makes something lovely of it all— like the less-than-perfect school costume this father hand-sewed for his overjoyed litle girl. In His time, He makes *all* things beautiful.

PRAYER: *Father, You hold my present, past, and future in Your loving hands, especially* (name your hardest present circumstance). *Thank You that in Your time, even this will become beautiful.*

Great expectations

⸙

READ PHILIPPIANS 2:1-5.
"Do not merely look out for your own personal interests, but also for the interests of others."
Philippians 2:4

When Christmas is your favorite season, not even a houseful of company and a dependent relative can dampen your excitement. One year we bought a two-foot Christmas tree for my mother-in-law's room. After securing it on top of her bureau we trimmed it with twinkling lights, tiny balls, and tinsel.

Everyone was up early on Christmas morning. My husband lit the fire while I poured orange juice and coffee, then heated orange rolls I'd baked the week before. We helped Penny into her recliner, snuggled her with blankets and pillows, and wheeled her into the living room. Despite her senile dementia, we knew she'd never forget this cozy Christmas.

But in less than an hour the animated conversation, piles of wrapping paper, and unfamiliar food had exhausted her. "Can I go back to bed now?" she asked, her face pale. She spent the rest of the day there, picking at Christmas dinner from a tray across her lap.

Two agendas collided that holiday morning: Penny's and mine. Hers was bordered by the limits of her illness and need for quiet. Mine sprang from fairy tale memories and unreal expectations. That experience taught me to bathe every upcoming family activity in prayer. Is there a special event on your horizon? Have you prayerfully balanced your own expectations with reality?

PRAYER: Oh Father, so much is expected of me. Give me discernment as I minister to those You have entrusted to my care.

Silence is golden

∞

READ PSALM 62.
"My soul waits in silence for God only; from Him is my salvation." Psalm 62:1

"He's never quiet," despaired a weary mother of a developmentally disabled child. "He talks all the time, usually with words and syllables that don't make sense. He bangs on things constantly. . . ."

"Would you let me stay with him tomorrow afternoon, while you get away?"

She stared at her friend, shaken. "Oh . . . it's really hard. I never know what he'll do next . . . I couldn't ask you to do that. . . ."

"If you'll tell me what to do, I'm willing to give it a try."

How's your own level of noise tolerance? Does your relative's television run eight hours or more a day? Does he shout when you walk by? Must the other children play quietly, lest they disturb your one precious hour of peace while he naps? Is the tension in your home crackling so loud it hurts your ears?

Has a friend offered to relieve you? Have you been hesitant to accept that help? For the success of your soul's health, allow yourself a second look at that offer. Then give yourself a few hours alone—when nobody will need you, nobody will call your name. Listen to the Psalmist, and somehow, somewhere, discover a way to spend quiet time alone with God.

PRAYER: *Father, thank You for speaking to me in the silent places. Please help me to listen for Your voice, especially during* (name the time you and God will be alone).

An alien love

___

READ DEUTERONOMY 10:17-21.
"So show your love for the alien, for you were aliens in the land of Egypt." Deuteronomy 10:19

I don't want any!"
"Just try a bite or two, Kevin. I beat the eggs with a little water, the way we all like . . . ."

"No! I don't want them!" Before I could stop him, two-year-old Kevin splattered a mouthful of scrambled eggs on the carpet.

I murmured something about "maybe tomorrow," scooping up pieces of egg with a paper napkin. Kevin forgot about the breakfast episode in minutes, but I couldn't. Running a day-care for three children was challenging enough without one of Kevin's bad days.

Probably his father didn't come home again last night. Kevin's mother did her best to hold down a job and raise three children. But she couldn't provide the one thing her strong-willed son needed: the consistent love and discipline of his father. I understood the home situation, but on days like this that wasn't enough. What was I supposed to do with Kevin?

"So show your love for the alien," instructs today's Scripture. On his obstinate days Kevin seemed an alien. Often I felt I didn't know him. And sometimes I didn't want to. "For you were aliens in the land of Egypt," the passage continues. When I was unlovable, Christ gave Himself for me. When I was an alien, He loved what He knew me to be. I can do no less.

PRAYER: *Sometimes I don't recognize the one I'm caring for, Lord. Flood me today with love for this stranger I often don't understand, especially* (name the alien in your family at the moment).

21

Opening tired eyes

✂

READ JAMES 1:17-18.
*"Every good thing bestowed and every perfect
gift is from above . . ." James 1:17*

W e are so tired," a caregiving daughter
1,500 miles away sighed during a Saturday morning phone call. Her voice trembled as
she recounted her nearly blind father's surgery
for colon cancer. Six days had passed, during
which he nearly died. Now he was out of intensive care, but long months of difficult convales-
cence lay ahead.

"All the decisions . . . it's exhausting. So two
nights ago on the spur of the moment Mark
and I made up our minds to grill dinner on the
beach. Dad would be all right—and we needed
some time out!"

Her voice became animated as she recounted

the evening. "The friends we called were able to meet us, and guess what happened? While we were eating, a school of dolphins entertained us in the moonlight for an hour and a half! It was God's serendipity gift to us!"

A caregiving season can go on for months—even years—without changing. Inevitable crises can compress memories and decisions into hours, leaving the caregiver numb with fatigue. Yet whatever is taking place, God never turns away. His open hand stretches toward us, casting no shadow. One day at a time He sends a serendipity present to every caregiver: a blooming yellow rose, a child's sweet kiss, graceful dolphins arching into a silver sea. Look around. What present has He sent you, special delivery, just for today?

PRAYER: *Father I see; yet I too am blind. Touch my eyes, Lord, that I may recognize the blessings of this day.*

The Gospel according to you

———— ∽ ————

READ II TIMOTHY 4:17-18.
"... in order that through me the proclamation
might be fully accomplished ..."
II Timothy 4:17a

Why did this happen to us ... why?" In
one way or another most of us can
understand this man's despair as his wife bat-
tled a brain tumor.

Whether caring for a husband, wife, parent,
or child, the often bleak present stands in
stark contrast to the remembered past. No
words can bridge the gap between what used
to be, and now is. No words can describe the
pain of watching a beloved family member
deteriorate.

Why did this happen to us ... to you?
Paul's second letter to Timothy suggests one

answer often overlooked. Paul, imprisoned and facing death, states that "the Lord stood with me and strengthened me, in order that . . ." Those last three little words provide the clue: God fortified Paul *in order that* through the testimony of his life the proclamation of the Gospel might be fully accomplished.

Did you ever think of parenting or caring for your loved one as an opportunity to proclaim the Gospel of Christ? Each person who enters your home sees a brand new picture of God at work, even in the midst of your most difficult circumstances.

God is using your faithful care, your patience, your honesty, even your painful questions to His glory. Today as time allows, take a prayer walk through every room of your home. Ask God to use every inch of it, right in the midst of today's greatest challenges, to His glory.

PRAYER: Father, I am so tired. Open my eyes, Lord, that I may see You at work in these circumstances You have allowed.

Mercy, pure and simple

∽

READ MATTHEW 5:1-16.
"Blessed are the merciful, for they shall receive mercy." Matthew 5:7

Nurse, could you come over here? There's something I want to show you. . . ."

My patient, who rarely said so many words at one time, sounded worried. I put away my pen and hurried to her chair.

"It's these things," she told me, extending her hands, palms down. "See? It's all these red marks . . . they look awful!"

She was right. Her care plan stated that over the last year angry, purple-red bruises had appeared on the tissue-paper skin of her hands. They formed after the slightest knock or pressure, and would not go away. The doctor explained that her failing circulation was

the indirect cause. Other than trying to pre-
vent them, there was nothing more to do.

"I wish we could get rid of them." She
stroked the shaking fingers of one hand over
the other.

I watched her, searching my mind. "We just
got some new lotion. They may not disappear
overnight, but it might help."

Her deep brown eyes lit up as I brought a
new bottle of rich emollient lotion to her room,
and she spent many minutes massaging it into
her skin. "I think it's working already!" she
exclaimed.

Mercy rarely wears dress clothes. It appears
humbly, clothed in a gentle word, a tender
hug, a three-dollar bottle of soothing lotion.
What kind of clothes will your loved one see
you wearing today?

**PRAYER: Thank You, Lord, for simplicity.
Sharpen my eyes and ears to the uncompli-
cated solutions all around me.**

The kindest of gifts

∽

READ COLOSSIANS 3:12-17.
". . . put on a heart of compassion, kindness, humility, gentleness and patience . . ."
Colossians 3:12

"Grandma, why're you crying?" Rita had helped her grandmother eat, shower, and dress, and looked forward to a few errands before lunch.

"I'm sorry dear," she murmured, dabbing at her eyes. "I thought you were gone. You shouldn't have to worry about such things."

"Grandma, do you hurt somewhere?"

The frail, white haired woman smiled faintly. "Not on the outside. It's the memories. It's all so silly . . . so long ago."

"Like when?"

"It was during World War I, and my father

was away in the Navy. My mother left me to watch my baby sister, your great aunt Eleanor, but I cut out paper dolls instead. She climbed onto a window ledge and fell off. Her arm never did heal right." She twisted a soggy tissue with shaking hands.

"Grandma, how old were you then?"

"Oh, about seven. Mom needed me so much, but I let her down. . . ."

"Tell you what. If I make us a cup of tea, would you tell me some more about those years? There's a lot I'd like to know."

Kindness slips an invisible arm around all kinds of pain. And often that means finding time for a desperately needed talk, even about things that happened three-quarters of a century ago.

PRAYER: *Forgive me, Lord, for my preoccupation with activity. Help me to take time today to give the gift of a listening ear, especially to* (add the name of the most difficult person in your life).

Anticipating our needs

ငာ

READ ISAIAH 65:21-24.
"Before they call, I will answer; and while they are still speaking, I will hear." Isaiah 65:24

"After retirement we'd always planned to travel, so we sold our house and bought the motor home," explained a wife whose husband had cancer. "We never dreamed something like this would happen. We miss our old home and children so much, but that's not the hardest part."

"It's difficult to imagine what could be much worse," I admitted, glad my vacation had allowed me to visit her.

"The hardest part is that we know so few people here. We need our own support team of friends and neighbors. We feel so isolated struggling with tough decisions about his care."

As I searched for encouraging words she suddenly laughed. "We'd prayed about how alone we felt, and guess what happened? During Tom's recovery from surgery I ran into four people I actually did know—all in one afternoon! One even took time to pray with me in the waiting room."

"Before they call," today's reading promises, "I will answer; and while they are still speaking, I will hear." Are you worried or uncomfortable about a situation in your family? Is there a feeling, or perhaps something you know you need to do, that makes you uneasy? Write it down, and today take that need to God in specific prayer. While you are still speaking, He will answer.

PRAYER: *Father, how often I forget to bring every concern, great and small, before You. Help me remember to first call to You, and then to listen for Your answer.*

Earning the Master's praise

⎯⎯⎯ ∞ ⎯⎯⎯

READ MATTHEW 25:14-26.
"Well done, good and faithful slave; you were
faithful with a few things, I will put you in
charge of many things . . ." Matthew 25:21

Did you plant a garden last spring? Or perhaps set some colorful clay pots or wooden
tubs outside? Whatever the project, it's fun
when you've assembled everything you're going
to need: soil enricher, fertilizer, a trowel, a
rake, some other tools, and healthy new plant
starts from the nursery or seedbed. Each step
of the undertaking flows logically from the one
before it. Though it's time consuming and hard
work, what you need is all in one place and the
job rarely seems difficult.

But twenty-four hour responsibility for
someone else doesn't come together so neatly.

You try to think ahead, but each new day brings challenges impossible to prepare for. You assemble supplies ahead of time for baths, diaper or dressing changes, feedings, and outings. Yet inevitably you overlook the one thing you really need. And though plants from the nursery don't want to talk or play, the one you're caring for probably does, slowing the task you're trying to finish.

Efficiency and proper equipment make any chore easier. But Jesus puts a different quality at the top of any project evaluation list: faithfulness. He reserves the highest praise for those who loyally carry out their job with the tools at hand. The Lord won't ask if you were organized and skillful. He will ask only one question: were you faithful?

PRAYER: *I complain too much, Lord, most of all because I don't have* (add your own word or phrase). *Help me this day to faithfully use the talents and resources You have already provided.*

A break in the action

―――――――――― ∽ ――――――――――

READ PSALM 23.
"The Lord is my shepherd, I shall not want."
Psalm 23:1

I had the most wonderful time yesterday," a new mother exclaimed. "I was only away from home six hours, but it seemed like six days!" Her eyes hadn't been so bright in months.

"Tell me everything you did," I urged.

"I started early with the aerobics class I'd been putting off—that was a good feeling. Then I took myself out for lunch and read a novel the whole time! Next, I went shopping, and later on I went to the snack bar for tea and a muffin, and planned more shopping!"

"Did all that tire you out?"

"No. It was wonderful!"

How about you? How do you feel today?

What have you planned to do? How long since you had a day off? Would you enjoy six whole hours to yourself . . . maybe more? Jesus, who alone knows your heart, desires that you lack nothing, including time to become the person He created you to be.

Though time away may look impossible, begin right now to pray about it. Ask the Lord to show you someone who can stay with the one you care for. Then make plans to lie down for a while in green pastures, to walk beside still waters—in whatever form means the most to you. God understands the longings of your heart, the pressured fatigue of your body. Right now, ask Him to lead you to a time and place of refreshment.

PRAYER: *Oh Father, I do so need some time away. Show me how that can happen, so that You may restore my soul.*

Getting a grip on isolation

————— ∞ —————

READ ISAIAH 49:14-16.
"Behold, I have inscribed you on the palms of My hands." Isaiah 49:16a

Have you ever stood in a crowd of people and felt utterly alone? In coliseums, airports, and even in shopping malls everyone seems to have something to do, a place to go, a schedule to keep. People glance at you without seeing, and rush on. You tell yourself it's silly to feel so alone. If you called out they'd surely answer . . . wouldn't they?

Like those places designed to serve huge numbers of people, taking care of a tiny baby, a child, or someone else also has an uneven rhythm. Your routine remains the same for months, even years. Then in an instant something goes wrong, shattering the predictable harmony of your days.

During such times you may wonder, however briefly, if God has forgotten you. Can't-do, must-do, when-there's-time-to-do and try-to-do lists surround you. And right in the middle of it all you feel completely isolated.

Take a minute right now to look at your palms and the tips of your fingers. See the swirls and lines that make your handprint one-of-a-kind? In today's reassuring Scripture God explains that the palms of His hands contain something more; on them He has written your name. In loneliness and frightening change He has forever promised, "I will not forget you." He has made you a part of Himself.

PRAYER: *Father, I am overwhelmed to realize You have inscribed me on the palm of Your hand. When I feel most alone, help me to rest there, secure in the strong grip of Your love.*

Learning to sing again

READ PSALM 33:1-8.
"Sing to Him a new song, play skillfully with a shout of joy." Psalm 33:3

"W here's Randy? He's not in the backyard . . . ." Her voice trembles.

"Did you check in front?"

"But he couldn't be out there. I locked the side gate."

They rush through the front door, desperate to find the son whose once handsome head was pierced ten years ago by a bullet from a friend's rifle.

"Oh Sam," she whispers, hot tears stinging her tired eyes.

Thirty-year-old Randy, long ago a cross-country racer, sits on the edge of the curb. He grips a pair of pruning shears, methodically cutting tiny pieces from a dried branch into a rusty coffee can.

"I gave him his hand weights . . ."

"He's not interested in those, honey. He wants to be active."

Has an injury ended the song your loved one used to sing? Does the woman who won blue ribbons for her apple pie now eat it with her hands? Does the young man who outran the wind now cut up old branches by the side of the road?

Former abilities may be gone, but your loved one can sing new songs to the Lord. What substitutes can you fashion from yesterday's talents? Could the baker place presliced apples into a preformed crust? Could the racer meet strong friends who laugh with him as they chase the wind together? Ask, and God will teach you to create new music from a minor key.

PRAYER: O Lord, put a new song in my mouth. Please teach me to see challenges instead of problems.

Words we long to hear

———— ∞ ————

READ PROVERBS 25:8-15.
"Like apples of gold in settings of silver is a word spoken in right circumstances."
Proverbs 25:11

Our guide through a turn-of-the-century mansion stopped in front of a brightly lit case built into the paneled wall. "The dining room was set up to seat thirty or more people at a time," she explained.

Using a small key to unlock the glass door of the display case, she reached inside and lifted out two silver water goblets. The glowing silver flowed delicately into a solid base, and I strained to see more.

"Each of these was monogrammed in gold with the family's initial," she continued, rotating them toward us. The light streaming from the window across the room splashed over the burnished silver, backlighting the graceful letter's golden patina. Enchanted, I drank in the symmetry and strength combined into such works of art.

Just as I immersed myself in the beauty I saw that day, parents also need to bathe from time to time in the sound of encouraging words. Their work continues for weeks, months, and years, during which many hear little more than "Why? When? How come?"

Has God placed someone in your life whose words you especially long to hear? Could you phone or visit that person, and treat yourself to an hour or so of understanding conversation? Why not contact him or her today, and make plans to spend a little time together? Allow the Lord to encourage you this week through that tailor-made friend He has provided.

PRAYER: *Father, sometimes I feel as if my spirit has prickly heat. Help me to phone (add your friend's name) this week.*

Making the necessary changes

⁓

READ PSALM 102:1-12.
"Hear my prayer, O Lord! And let my cry for help come to Thee." Psalm 102:1

How many psychiatrists does it take to change a light bulb?"

"Only one—but the light bulb has to be willing to change."

Probably without intending to, that silly little joke illustrates a profound spiritual truth. Even if a battalion of electricians surrounds the light bulb, nothing will change unless the bulb allows it.

How's your attitude been lately? Do you feel like a hamster stuck on a revolving wheel, with no way to get off? Are you, as one friend described himself, a "basket case"? Have you recently shouted angry, hurtful words at the people dearest to you? Has the joy of your salvation, not to mention everything else, all but disappeared?

Your anguish probably calls for several solutions, some highly practical. Are you insisting on some time alone each day? Are you talking to friends, searching for a small group, carving out at least some relief? Are you getting enough rest? If you answered no to one or more of these questions, you may be a lot like the light bulb—desperately in need of change, but not yet willing to allow that to happen.

Prayerfully reread Psalm 102, focusing on each word. If you feel like crying, give in to it. Allow the Holy Spirit to ease the tensions you feel. He longs to do so much in your specific situation. Right now, ask Him to make you willing to change.

PRAYER: *Father, You know that some of my relationships desperately need help, especially (add your own words). Teach me to listen for Your voice, and then be willing to obey what you tell me.*

Heaven's scent

───────────────── ✂ ─────────────────

READ II CORINTHIANS 2:14-17.
"For we are a fragrance of Christ . . ."
II Corinthians 2:15

I grew up in a canyon near the Pacific Ocean. For over half the year geraniums, poppies, nasturtiums, and wildflowers spread their brilliant colors over its sunny walls. One day as my sister and I hiked to the remote end of the narrow valley we discovered the most beautiful flower of all: a single rosebush that stretched for more than half a block.

Its gnarled trunk supported branches covered with dainty, pale pink roses. Hundreds of its full-blown flowers bloomed alongside tender, bright pink buds. Though their stems rarely exceeded four inches in length, the scent of those roses attracted us long before we saw them.

For years we trekked to that bush on Mother's Day, to pick dozens of the small buds and carry them home in a basket. There we secretly arranged them into nosegays edged with paper doilies, and encircled our mother's place at the dinner table with the fragrant blooms.

When I had my own family of children I thought wistfully of those delicate roses. Did my parenting reflect the Lord Jesus? The roses' sweet scent attracted my sister and me, even before they came into view. Were my words and actions at home that same aroma of Christ to my family?

I knew the answer was often no. But far more times I sensed it was yes, as I trusted Jesus to draw my children closer to Himself through me. How are mealtimes in your home? Bedtimes? Sundays? Ask God to help you reflect Him in the midst of each chore you do today.

PRAYER: *Take my everyday tasks, Lord, and transform them. Help the care I give my family today to be a sweet aroma of You.*

Doubt-filled diplomacy

⟶ ∽ ⟵

READ MATTHEW 7:7-11.
"Ask, and it shall be given to you; seek, and
you shall find; knock, and it shall be opened to
you." Matthew 7:7

"Before I go out to play, Mom, I'm going to clean my room."

Our nine year old's words froze my feet to the floor. At our house room cleaning never happened voluntarily.

"Think I'll do the bathroom, too."

I moved to the doorway of his room to see if he looked feverish. He didn't. "Is there something you'd like to talk about?" I asked.

"Well, sort of. There's batting practice at the new club later, and I wondered if I could go . . ." he hesitated, "after I've cleaned my room."

Today's Scripture is as direct as our son

could have been with me, had he realized it. I was all in favor of batting practice—he had only to ask. Instead he chose a subtle strategy, afraid I'd say no.

How often we experiment with the same tactics when it comes to prayer. We bargain: "If You do this, Lord, I promise I'll do that." We beat around the bush, whitewashing needs and desires God already knows all about, simply because we are His children.

He longs for us to come directly to Him in believing prayer. "Ask," He says simply. "Seek," He encourages us. "Knock, and it shall be opened to you," He promises. He holds no hoops we must jump through, no litany of prerequisites. We are to keep asking, keep seeking, keep knocking. He will do the rest.

PRAYER: *My single greatest need today, Father, is (add your own words). Help me to recognize the door You will open for me.*

To heal and be healed

―――――――― ∽ ――――――――

READ ISAIAH 6:1-8.
"Then I said, 'Here am I. Send me!'"
Isaiah 6:8b

"Isn't working here hard for you?" a friend
asked over a hurried lunch. "Aren't you
angry a lot? It seems as if I feel that way most
of the time!" She laughed, brushing away tears
with the back of her hand.

I described the fatigue, frustration, and
hurry that characterized my first few months
in the job I used to think was ideal. I told her
of my smoldering anger as my boss's demands
heaped one pressure on another. I detailed the
pain of our relationship, the threat I believed
she saw in me. I confided that I used to feel I
was the last person on earth she would have
chosen, had she done the hiring.

"Then how can you keep on?" she asked, slowly shaking her head.

Answering that wasn't hard. One day I'd found my boss crying, and could almost hear the Lord asking, "Whom shall I send, and who will go for Us?" I'd been thinking of quitting, but I knew the Lord had my name on His list. He understood that my boss and I both needed healing. That long process began when I answered, "Here am I. Send me!"

Is your employment situation less than ideal? In spite of that, do you feel God has called you, at least for now, to work there? Healing will flow from your obedience to that call. In the midst of confusion and misunderstanding, God is refining your employer, your co-workers and you.

PRAYER: *I don't really understand why You have called me to this work, Lord. But I accept it, despite my frequent problems with (add your own words). Thank You that absolutely no situation, no relationship, lies beyond Your healing touch.*

It's hard to be firm

_____ ∞ _____

READ PSALM 32:6-11.
"I will instruct you and teach you in the way which you should go." Psalm 32:8a

I have constant headaches, my faith is weakening, my marriage is in trouble. . . . I don't know what to do!" My friend, who five years before had taken in her unemployed brother's family, pressed a napkin to her mouth.

"If you could have one wish, what would it be?" I asked.

"To have my house back," she whispered.

Most shelter ministries aren't meant to last forever. Often the Lord calls His people to help adult children or other family members for a season. Then like dried autumn leaves drifting earthward, He sends gentle signals that their hospitality assignment is ending. Perhaps their relatives require things the home can no longer offer. Perhaps the host has been stretched to the breaking point.

Selecting alternatives is never easy, rarely quick and simple. It requires persistent phone calls, endless networking, and loving firmness with relatives often unable to understand its complex, painful realities.

Is it time for someone you love to seek other solutions? Does the thought of it overwhelm you? In today's psalm the Lord pledges to instruct you as you weigh every option, to lead you to the best path for you and your loved one's unique situation, to watch over your progress, and to advise you all along the way. He will bear the pain of this search with you, and infuse every decision with His love. But the first step is up to you.

PRAYER: *Though this process hurts so much Lord, I must begin. Because You are beside me, today I will* (add your first step).

Beyond control

ക

READ EPHESIANS 6:10-18.
"Therefore, take up the full armor of God, that you may be able to resist in the evil day, and having done everything, to stand firm."
Ephesians 6:13

Look Grandma, I see two trains coming!"
Three-year-old Alesha waved her small hands in the air then crouched down, laughing.

"The engineer's waving back at you. See him?"

"I want the one on the other tracks to wave too, Grandma! You can make him do it. Hurry, Grandma, he's going by!"

He did indeed go by, and both trains soon streaked from sight. Our grandaughter's sunshine smile hid behind clouds for several minutes as I tried to explain my inability to control fast trains and busy engineers.

When I was a
Alesha—so totally
pening that I assu
would agree to do
time before I accep
traveled on one set
As much as I might
not—and should not-
choices different from
my own were separate.

As painful as that pr⋯ ⋯ of acceptance
was, it proved to be wonderfully freeing. Having completed everything I believed she required and needed, I could lovingly move on with my life. I had prayed, worked, and done all I knew to do for her. God was in complete control. He did not need my intervention to work in Penny's life—or in my own.

PRAYER: *Thank You, Lord, that You are God. Help me to remember that my loved one's life, and mine, are separate. Today I relinquish (add your loved one's name), and her (his) choices, to You.*

ssoming in life's shadows

∽

READ PSALM 17:6-8.
"Hide me in the shadow of Thy wings."
Psalm 17:8b

One Sunday last summer my husband and I went to church, then treated ourselves to an afternoon of backyard gardening. We trimmed spent iris blooms, sprayed roses, weeded flower beds, and watered the pots of pink and white petunias.

All afternoon the fourteen pine trees in our yard created broad splashes of sun and shade. But this didn't seem to bother the plants at all. Roses, petunias, marigolds, and snapdragons thrived in the bright sun. In the cool shadows nearby other plants flourished with equal abandon: waxy white begonias, dainty impatiens, graceful columbine.

Wherever they were rooted, God provided continous growth for each plant. Maybe you're feeling a little like a shade plant today, and wonder if you're growing at all. Like rosebushes, most of us equate growth with comfort and warmth. We forget that God delights to use every event, every condition of our lives to produce the blossoms He desires.

Today's verse implores the Lord to hide its writer in the shadow of His wings. There the psalmist knows he will be in his heavenly Father's embrace. Parenting brings difficult choices and decisions, and it helps to thank God for those shadowy times. Through them He mysteriously draws us to Himself, cultivating spiritual growth as varied and beautiful as flowers on a hot summer day. What special challenge do you face today?

PRAYER: *Father, thank You for allowing the circumstances that cause me to grow. By faith I accept them, and their spiritual harvest as yet hidden from my sight.*

Restoring a healthy perspective

∞

READ LAMENTATIONS 3:22-25.
*"The Lord is good to those who wait for Him, to
the person who seeks Him." Lamentations 3:25*

After his bypass surgery, our daughter Ann
and I brought my husband home from
the hospital in early April. Four months later,
we managed our first vacation. As Gus backed
the car out of the driveway I remember leaning
my head against the seat, my eyes closed,
unable to grasp the reality of four whole days
to ourselves.

We drove north into western Canada, our
destination the historic old mining town of Nel-
son. During that never-to-be-forgotten holiday
the three of us renewed ourselves beside
Kootenay Lake, surrounded by the green-gray
arms of the Selkirk Mountains.

At first, consumed by enormous need, we

discussed the changes his illness had carved into our lives. But as the restful hours washed over us we talked less, relieved by the slow, restorative pace of vacation. We returned home in late afternoon of the fourth day, already making plans for our next getaway. The Lord restored each one of us from the inside out, and we resumed our daily lives with a fresh perspective.

How long has it been since you had some time away from the load you carry? Could you manage a few days, or even a few hours, to seek and wait for the Lord to renew you? Would you take a moment to pray about it right now? God is faithful above all else, and He will provide a way.

PRAYER: Thank You, Father, that Your compassions never fail. Show me how I can draw apart, no matter how short the time, to be refreshed by You.

Bearing weakness, sharing strength

⌘

READ ROMANS 15:1-6.
"Now we who are strong ought to bear the
weaknesses of those without strength. . . ."
Romans 15:1

One month after her first son turned two,
Deana Stolz delivered triplet baby boys.
She felt as if her life would be on overdrive forever, and she was probably right. Her days
raced by: dashing to the grocery store. Convinced she'd lost control of her own house.
Falling asleep in parking lots and church. And
never, ever caught up with the work.

Then a few months later Deana and her
husband Wade discovered one of the triplets
had a mild form of cerebral palsy, and their
lives grew even more complicated. Into their
impossibly crowded schedule they must now fit

physical therapy sessions, daily patterning exercises, medical evaluations, and extra stimulation. The care Jason receives each day will determine if he walks in the future.

"Everything seems so complicated," Deana says. "Just getting them all into the car takes half an hour. But we don't mind, because what we're doing is so important. The others don't understand, and we play with them all we can. But Jason needs help now, and he has nobody but us. We're dealing with it day by day, with God's help and guidance."

Do you have a reserve tank of strength today—enough to share with someone who needs help, like Wade and Deana? Think about your church family, your neighbors, the people under your own roof. Could you spare a little of that extra health and energy, and lighten their heavy load?

PRAYER: Take my hands and make them Yours, Lord. Open my eyes to the needs everywhere around me—even in my own home.

Our inadequacy,
His opportunity

―――――――――― ∽ ――――――――――

READ MATTHEW 14:14-21.
"And they all ate, and were satisfied."
Matthew 14:20a

She needs the antibiotic every four hours
around the clock. And getting moisture into
the air is vital. Do you have a vaporizer?" The
office nurse looked up, her pen poised over the
chart.

"Not anymore, but her grandfather and I
could get one."

"Good. As soon as possible. She should be
turned every two hours, to keep fluid from pool-
ing in her lungs. Now let's review her diet. . . ."

I nodded but heard little, my eyes on our
grandaughter's labored breathing from bron-
chitis. After examining her, our doctor encouraged us to continue caring for Lauren until her

parents returned from vacation. "They'd do nothing in the hospital you can't do," she reassured us.

Back home, I stood beside her bed for a long time. Only a year old, she appeared so small and weak and needed so much. I looked over the nurse's printed treatment list, felt utterly inadequate, and begged God for wisdom. Suddenly Lauren's cough racked her body and instinctively I helped her turn to one side, then held her until it subsided.

What I did that cold January morning became symbolic. One by one I yielded my insufficient skills and resources to Jesus. One by one He blessed them, used them, multiplied them. And each day Lauren grew stronger. As the Lord once fed five thousand people with the five loaves and two fish they gave Him, He turned my yielded little into much. God longs to use everything you and I possess—but first we must let go.

PRAYER: Lord, I surrender my meager abilities to You. Take, bless, and multiply them to Your glory.

God gives, even when life takes

———— ∽ ————

READ ZECHARIAH 9:9-12.
"This very day I am declaring that I will restore double to you." Zechariah 9:12b

"One for you, and one for me," my childhood friend crooned, cradling a giant sack of lemon drops from her doting grandmother.

We were best friends, but as we sat cross-legged on her driveway that sunny afternoon I kept track of every move she made. I couldn't bear to think of having fewer candies than she did, best friend or not.

Depending on how long you've been a working single parent, you may feel as if someone counted out the goodies and you came up short. Possibly many of the things you value have disappeared from your life:

Bible study, summer days at the lake, spontaneous anything.

Today's passage of Scripture is a stirring prophecy of Christ's first and second advent. But on another level, verses eleven and twelve seem to have been written for single parents. God promises that He will set the prisoners free and return them to the fortress. And there is even more. He promises to renew and rebuild their broken lives.

Have the pressures of raising children by yourself and holding down a full-time job shriveled the treasures in your life? Have they drained the laughter from your voice? Do you often feel like crying, remembering what might have been? God understands those secret thoughts, the times of sadness that wash over you like waves. He knows, He cares, and He is working powerfully on your behalf this very moment.

PRAYER: Take my hand, and lead me through this day, Lord. Teach me to laugh again, especially with my family.

The healing art of listening

———————— ∞ ————————

READ PROVERBS 23:22-25
"Listen to your father who begot you . . . and let her rejoice who gave birth to you."
Proverbs 23:22-25

I'm so interested in all this!" My patient point-ed at the newspaper.

"What were you reading?" I asked, hoping we might talk about it.

For a moment her eyes held mine, and I glimpsed fear's shadow far within them. Then her awareness withered, replaced by a vacant stare. "Well," she began valiantly, "I'm not sure . . . but it's . . . it's. . . ." She waved an uncertain hand in the air and looked down, defeated.

My heart ached as I knelt beside her, feigning recognition and shared awareness of the headline story. Alzheimer's disease had robbed her of memory and understanding, but she still longed to exchange ideas. That morning I listened to her on two levels: pretending to discuss an unidentified story, while asking God to reveal what my patient really wanted. I discovered that most of all, she needed simple reassurance.

Of all the tools available to those who care for others, perhaps listening is the most valuable of all. As with my patient that morning, what is said doesn't really matter. But how it is received is priceless.

Using two ears isn't enough. Gentle silence, a soft touch, a nod of the head, warm eye contact, and laughter are all a part of real listening. Have you learned the healing art of hearing beyond the spoken word? Take note of your conversations today. Who does most of the talking? The listening?

PRAYER: *Father, thank You for hearing not just my words but my heart. Teach me to listen with Your patient and understanding love.*

First aid for wounded hearts

⎯⎯⎯⎯⎯ ∞ ⎯⎯⎯⎯⎯

READ JAMES 5:13-16.
"Confess your sins to one another."
James 5:16a

Though three-and-a-half-year-old Katie didn't feel well, she still managed to play and make a mess. Before serving lunch her mother urged her to pick up her puzzles, blocks, and dolls.

When Katie refused she was sent to her room to think it over. A few minutes later she opened the bedroom door. "I'm sorry Mom," she said. "I'm just not myself today."

How are things going in your family? Like Katie, have you not been yourself lately? Have you used angry words as a weapon, loathing the sound of them but unable to stop? Or perhaps seized a far more painful tactic—silence?

Have you shouted in anger or done other things you're ashamed of, things that burn in your memory like a branding iron?

Katie modeled a good starting place to shed remorse. She said she was sorry. If words, or silence, or something worse have injured someone in your family, or perhaps another person, begin by telling them how much you regret what happened.

The next step comes from today's Bible reading. Within this familiar passage, verse 16 is sometimes overlooked. It tells us to confess our sins to one another, and to pray for each other. Why? So that we may be healed. Today, ask God for a friend you can confide in, one who will pray faithfully for your strengths—and weaknesses. Then meet with that friend regularly. Talk, confess, pray together, and God will heal.

PRAYER: *Forgive me, Lord, for the ways I have failed You. And then, Father, please help me to forgive myself.*

No unmet need is too small

———— ∽ ————

READ PHILIPPIANS 4:18-23.
"And my God shall supply all your needs
according to His riches in glory in Christ Jesus."
Philippians 4:19

"You're getting a what?" a friend asked our daughter.

"A three-month-old puppy!"

"But you're taking care of an incontinent baby—how can you handle an incontinent puppy?" Skepticism bounced from every word.

"I don't know," Leslie admitted. With Teddy only three months old, Lee and Leslie knew that a puppy made no sense at all.

But their hearts ruled, and the chocolate lab they named Cocoa proved to be one of their top parenting decisions. He lived to please them, watching everything they did with patient and understanding brown eyes. "I love Teddy so much," Leslie confided, "but I miss my job, and getting out, and meeting people." After Cocoa joined their family, his antics and daily walks soon introduced them to new friends and activities.

What small dream would bring sparkle to your daily routine, possibly something that makes little or no sense? Our daughter and her husband felt incomplete without a dog. Perhaps you're longing for something different—that only you can understand.

Whatever your need, God promises to supply it according to His riches in glory in Christ Jesus. Look into your heart right now. Can you identify the longing you find there? Tell the Lord about it, be patient—and get ready for joy.

PRAYER: Lord, thank You for caring so deeply about my smallest need. Today I reach out in faith, and whisper it to You.

Balm for the aching heart

———— ∞ ————

READ JEREMIAH 31:1-6.
"I have loved you with an everlasting love."
Jeremiah 31:3b

I fixed your favorite breakfast, Mom. Will you try a bite or two?"

The ninety-two-year-old woman turned her head away, tears flooding her pale, wrinkled cheeks.

"Mom, does something hurt? Can you tell me about it?" The frightened daughter leaned forward.

"I think you know the answer," her mother sobbed. "If only your brother would call. . . ."

Too familiar pain knotted the younger woman's stomach. She stood up, weary after two nights of fitful sleep as her mother's heart rhythm refused to regulate. Her brother had not visited nor phoned in nearly two months, but their mother wasn't counting. She hungered only for her son's presence, the one thing her daughter could not provide.

The caregiver offered a few bites of food, then trudged to the kitchen. Did her mother love her? Without question, though in over half a century it had never been said. Did she appreciate a fraction of the care lavished upon her? Probably not.

"I have loved you with an everlasting love," God sings to the parched earth of your soul. He loves you without reservation, for exactly who you are. He loves you so much He allowed His only Son to exchange His life for yours. Thirst no longer. Right now, take a few moments to luxuriate in the endless flow of your heavenly Father's love for *you*.

PRAYER: Oh Lord, only You know the aching void in my heart. Refresh me with the deep and sparkling streams of Your love.

Shelter in times of storm

∞

READ PSALM 107:28-38.
"He caused the storm to be still, so that the waves of the sea were hushed." Psalm 107:29

W e took half a day off yesterday," the mother of an adult son with AIDS lamented to her support group. "When we got back home, there were five messages on our answering machine—all from Hal."

"What did you do?"

"By then it was after ten, and he goes to sleep very early. But guess who phoned at five-thirty the next morning? He's twenty-six and he was crying, though we'd told him all about our few hours off, and left several phone numbers with him. He's so different now, and he needs us so much. We felt terrible, but we've got to have some time away!"

There are two halves in any parenting equation, even this one: the parents, and the one they're caring for. Balance between both is essential, and requires constant reassessment. But much too often, as with Hal and his parents, the dependent half of the equation stretches the relationship to the breaking point.

The Lord longs to transform all of your parenting areas—even those that may be stormy or tragic. Pray in faith, and He will provide help in simple ways: a new companion for your frightened loved one, or alternate housing, or twenty-four hour telephone reassurance. Today, are you, or someone you love, dealing with a heartbreaking situation? Be specific as you ask God for eyes to see the practical help He will provide.

PRAYER: *Father, sometimes the waves from caring for* (add your own words) *overwhelm me. Show me how to stay afloat, Lord.*

Beyond present horizons

———— ∞ ————

READ PSALM 19.
*"The heavens are telling of the glory of God;
and their expanse is declaring the work of His
hands." Psalm 19:1*

Perhaps no view is as breathtaking as that
from an orbiting spaceship. Astronauts
speak in hushed voices as they describe the
earth far beneath them. Like a bride's veil,
wispy clouds trail across mighty continents.
Over it all arches the endless midnight of outer
space. More than one astronaut has come to
personal faith in the Creator God from such a
view, stunned by heaven's declaration of the
awesome work of His hands.

But the spaceship must eventually return to
earth. And during that homeward journey, as
also in caring for small children, the traveler

must pass through a series of shrinking horizons. Two continents contract to one. Invisible mountains erupt where before there were none. A land mass shrivels to a nation, to a city, to a landing zone.

What kind of horizons encircle your parenting world? Are they limited to occasional trips to the mall or grocery store? Do you take the long way home, knowing that to stop is to end your baby's short nap?

Whatever boundaries parenting may have placed around your life, the laws and testimony and commandments of the Lord never change. Go to a window right now, and look at the skyline. In the fulness of God's time, your shrinking world will stretch to that horizon, and far beyond.

PRAYER: Thank You, Lord, that You are the same yesterday, today, and forever. Please show me new ways to mirror Your endless love to my family—at mealtime, bedtime, and through the day.

Celebration:
homemade therapy

READ PROVERBS 17:17-28.
"A joyful heart is good medicine."
Proverbs 17:22a

Hey, what's all this for?" Our son, a new Marine recruit, eyed the carmel icing swirled over his favorite chocolate cake.

"We're celebrating!"

"What's going on?"

"You're going into the Marines," his Dad explained as I placed the cake in front of him. "And are we proud!"

"All right! Is this German chocolate?"

The time sped by as I cut slices and scooped vanilla ice cream onto waiting plates. As we enjoyed it, everyone at the table focused on stories about Matt. Despite his upcoming departure from home he devoured three helpings, laughed with us, and even shared some of his feelings as Boot Camp neared. It was a celebration we've never forgotten.

Today's reading does more than recommend laughter. The Lord also makes clear its therapeutic value, akin to good medicine. What's coming up for someone in your family? Could you uncover an excuse for a celebration, however small in scope? It doesn't take much: a bouquet of fresh daisies delivered with a hug, a special dessert, homemade signs and streamers, a favorite meal, a cluster of balloons. Why not try your hand at working a family celebration into the days ahead? It costs next to nothing, and the memories last forever.

PRAYER: Open my eyes, Lord, to the family milestones all around me. Teach me to crown the art of homemaking with the art of celebration.

His presence in
the deepest valley

⌘

READ JOSHUA 1:1-9.
"Just as I have been with Moses, I will be with you; I will not fail you or forsake you."
Joshua 1:5b

How long do you plan to keep Annie home?" I asked a friend whose seven-year-old daughter would not live much longer.

"We'd like her with us the whole time, until . . ." she looked away.

"If it should go to the end," I asked gently, "will you be all right?"

"I . . . just the thought terrifies me, but I can't bear to think of her being anywhere else." She shook her head, pain engraved on her face.

Unless something changes, this mother's vigil will conclude with her daughter's death.

That hovering reality is one reason her ministry is so unspeakably difficult. Perhaps you are caring for someone you love beyond words. You may have had no prior experience with death. You don't know when it could come. You're afraid you'll be there when it happens. And you're afraid you won't.

Long ago the Lord called Joshua to a gigantic task: the conquest and division of Canaan. As a part of his marching orders God promised, over and over, never to fail or forsake him. If you face the possibility of a loved one's death, you may want to carve that soaring promise into your mind and heart.

Just as the Lord has been with you from the first day of your ordeal, so He will be with you through the last. He will meet every need you have. And whatever comes, He will never, ever leave your side.

PRAYER: The road ahead is strange Lord, and frightening. Thank You that I do not go alone, for You walk in lockstep beside me.

Turning problems
into picnics

━━━━━━━━━━━━━━ ᏇᎪ ━━━━━━━━━━━━━━

READ PSALM 78:14-20; 23-25.
"They said, 'Can God prepare a table in the wilderness?'" Psalm 78:19

When was the last time you went on a picnic? Maybe you and your friends walked a half block to a grassy park. Maybe you hiked a mile or more to a sandy beach at the foot of a granite cliff. Or maybe you shouldered your way through tall weeds to a sun-dappled river bank.

At last you reached your destination. "This looks nice," somebody said. "Shall we try it?" And then the sandy beach or riverbank or grassy slope was quickly transformed. An old quilt blanketed the ground. Tightly packed containers revealed chicken, fruit, salads, cookies, and much more.

Just as that picnic site came alive, God today seeks ways to prepare a table for you in the midst of your parenting. As you grasp a sticky hand, He teaches acceptance and understanding. As you answer the same question for the fifth time, He brings alive the art of patience.

Your insurmountable problem becomes His invitation to act. Through that very problem He will split the wilderness rocks blocking your spiritual growth. He will cause waters of joy to run down your life like rivers as you minister to your family.

What is the most formidable task you need to do today? The Lord will use that very challenge to provide grace you cannot dream of. Could you tackle that job right now, and allow God to bless you through it?

PRAYER: *As the picnic I remember once satisfied me Lord, lead me today to a spiritual table. Help me to view my hardest tasks, especially (add your own words), as an opportunity to grow in You.*

The triumph in our tears

———— ∞ ————

READ PSALM 126.
"Those who sow in tears shall reap with joyful shouting." Psalm 126:5

Late in our caregiving, cross words erupted between Bob and me one night. Finally something was said that caused me to drive to a nearby McDonald's restaurant. Food was the last thing on my mind. What I needed was time to sort out the reality of his mother's fast approaching death in our home.

I pulled between two pickups at the far end of the parking area, locked the doors, and leaned against the head rest. Then to my complete surprise I began to cry like an uncapped stream. Not a few tears, but a flooding torrent of grief, anger, exhaustion, and helplessness.

I remember sitting there in the semi-darkness, thinking how strange all this was, then feeling the tears overflow again as I remembered the electric tension at home. Twenty minutes later the emotional storm left as swiftly as it had arrived.

I drove home looking like a bedraggled puppy and spent needed time with Bob, describing the refreshment I had experienced. Though short on sleep, we faced the next morning and the days beyond girded for the three more weeks that would pass before his mother's peaceful death.

It felt good to cry that night, to stop being strong. Have tears tiptoed to the threshold of your emotions, only to be sent away? When they next return, allow them to stay. Through those tears God will cleanse and disperse the storm raging within you. And in His time, He pledges that you will reap with joyful shouting.

PRAYER: *You are familiar with sorrows, Lord, and acquainted with grief. Teach me to see tears as Your loving hand of renewal.*

What's in a touch?

⌘

READ EPHESIANS 4:1-6.
"Walk . . . with all humility and gentleness . . ."
Ephesians 4:1, 2

One bright morning of a much needed vacation, I strolled with our daughter Ann through a sloping meadow. Here and there jagged dandelion leaves sprouted, many silhouetted against the veined granite boulders native to the area. Their laughing yellow flowers flourished beside slender stems topped by round puffs of seed.

Ann picked one, sweeping the stem and its fragile contents around my head in a graceful arch. As the feathered seeds floated downward all around me, one grazed my face. I have never forgotten its softness, as touch and sight confirmed its drifting presence.

That tiny seed taught me much about my family. How gentle were my hands as I cared for them? Did my touch reassure each one of my committment and understanding? Did my eyes reflect love and belief in their potential? Were my words kind, my conversations patient, and did I search out ways to make them laugh?

"Nothing is so strong as gentleness; nothing so gentle as real strength," wrote St. Francis De Sales. As the gossamer dandelion seed hinted at the beauty within it, so gentleness conveys the indwelling Christ. As you care for each member of your family, how do you rate your eyes, your words, your touch? Take a quick inventory, remembering that tiny seed.

PRAYER: I reach up today, Lord, and grasp Your outstretched hand. Walk with me through all that I must do. Help me to slow down, and give You time to touch my family through me.

Knowing when to say when

ᏉᎷ

READ PSALM 4.
"The Lord hears when I call to Him." Psalm 4:3

I ache all over," sighed a single father of two as he grabbed the ringing phone.

"Won't keep you—just wanted to remind you of the men's work party at church tomorrow morning."

"Jim, this is hard to say, but right now I don't think I can keep that up. It's too much."

"That's too bad. We need to get that roof repaired before fall."

Have you been the target of similar multilevel messages? Without intending to, some family and friends view single parenting as an add-on instead of a highest priority ministry. They expect you at business and board meetings, work parties and planning sessions. They forget you also cook, wash, shop, attend teacher conferences, and occasionally sleep.

This expectation dilemma can be solved by the spiritual gift of discernment. You can't do a good parenting job and still respond to the agenda of everyone around you. If you try, you'll self-destruct.

Are you frazzled by unrealistic expectations? Today, ask the Holy Spirit to show you which activities should continue, and what should be put on hold. Ask Him also for the courage to be truthful with your friends and family. He has called you to the all-important ministry of parenting. He will give you abundant perception and judgment, that you may lovingly say yes to that call.

PRAYER: So many expect so much of me, Father. Show me today the things You would have me do, and those that can wait.

Caring begins on the inside

ᘓᘐ

READ PSALM 51:5-15.
"Thou dost desire truth in the innermost being,
and in the hidden part Thou wilt make me
know wisdom." Psalm 51:6

Saturday morning was wonderful," sighed
the mother of three little children, "until I
discovered the twins had been into my dresser.
One look and I told my husband I wanted a
lock on our bedroom door—right then."

"Was he able to do it?"

"He had one on in two hours and it's made
such a difference. It sounds awful to say, but
knowing I can get away for even a few minutes
has helped me relax."

Like this mother, are your own needs last on
your list? Do you feel guilty for wanting—and
desperately needing—some time and space for

yourself? Have you considered what would happen to your family if your marathon pace proves too much, and you hit the wall? Think it over.

In today's Psalm, David agonized before God over his sin of adultery. Failure to care for yourself, though by no means as serious, is nonetheless a sin. The Lord desires honesty from the heart. What are you holding back from Him? Do you need to prayerfully confess your failure to lovingly protect a few areas of your life? Do you need an occasional dinner alone with your husband? A few hours away each week? More privacy?

Right now, confess your self-neglect as the sin it is. Then ask your Heavenly Father to reveal those areas of your life in need of physical or emotional locks—and for the persistence and wisdom to apply them.

PRAYER: *Forgive me, Lord, for ignoring my own needs. Help me to remember that caring for anyone else begins with loving myself.*

Quality time

∽

READ JOHN 14:27-31.
"Let not your heart be troubled, nor let it be fearful." John 14:27

The six weeks between my mother's diagnosis of cancer and her death was one of the hardest in my life. Each day I drove across town to visit, not wanting to tire her but hungry to talk, to savor every possible moment together.

Those bittersweet hours pulsed with a fragile beauty. I discovered new dimensions of my mother's character, a quiet courage camoflaged by frequent laughter. One bright morning I brought her a small bouquet of strawberry pink carnations. Beaming, she inhaled their cinnamon-sweet scent. "I've always loved carnations!" she exclaimed. "They smell like the garden on a hot summer day."

Florist shop carnations and summer gardens were never again the same. To this day they remind me of my mother, of the joyful woman she was. Our restful conversations drift back to me on the patina of time, gifts from the Lord Who understood how much I would need them.

Perhaps you've been so caught up doing things for someone that you haven't had time for meaningful talk. Or perhaps your responsibilities serve as a pain killer, relieving the searing reality of what is happening. Would there be time this week for the two of you to say some things that need to be said? It will help more than you know. This very day, ask the Lord to give you an opportunity—and boldness. As you share together on a deeper level, He will flood the days ahead with His peace.

PRAYER: Lord, help me to slow down long enough to talk to (add a name). Please give me gentle speech and a listening ear.

Loving honesty

‿

READ EPHESIANS 4:7-16.
"But speaking the truth in love, we are to grow up in all aspects into Him, who is the head, even Christ." Ephesians 4:15

How're you doing?" Her brother's voice bounced through the phone.

"Oh, pretty well. We've all had summer colds. . . ." She selected her words carefully, thrown off guard after his six-month silence.

"Well, have we got a surprise for you! We thought we'd drop by during our family vacation. We've blocked out a whole week with you!"

"Well, uh . . . when do you think you might be arriving?"

"Who knows? We'll be on vacation time. We'll just show up!"

Today's reading from Ephesians encourages growing believers to learn to speak the truth in love. Uninvited guests provide an excellent place for Christian families to practice that. A whole week? Most parents go to the head of the class just for getting through the day.

How do you handle unexpected announcements of impending visitors? You may choose to firmly say no, urge staying in a motel, ask for a visit postponement, or say yes. Whatever your decision, pray for common sense and total honesty. Nobody understands your family situation except you.

You don't have to make excuses. God has called you to the ministry of raising a family. Ask Him, and He will teach you how to speak the truth in love—when that means a heartfelt "yes," and when it must mean a loving "no."

PRAYER: Lord, teach me the art of speaking the truth in difficult areas. And help me to make love the framework of my words.

Stop and smell the roses

———— ✍ ————

Read Psalm 8.
"O Lord, our Lord, how majestic is Thy name in all the earth." Psalm 8:1a

In many families, late afternoon opens a change-of-pace window on the day. Most of the work is over; dinner and the evening lie ahead. In our house the golden retriever seems to sense those transitional moments. He watches me with gentle eyes as I water pots of petunias, snip off dead blooms, and happily work my way through the restorative rituals of container gardening.

One late summer evening I picked a few flowers and carried them inside to our son Matt, home with the flu. Together we marveled at the fragile green stems supporting dainty blue lobelia. Four delicate petals, each less than a quarter of an inch, embraced the pure white centers. We wondered at a giant pansy, admiring the reds and purples that flowed from its compact yellow center.

Delighting in those diminutive flowers marvelously relaxed both Matt and me. Today's psalm rejoices in God's splendor reflected in heaven and earth. It draws a picture of majestic mountains and endless midnight sky. But those same verses speak also of God's wondrous, miniature creation: tiny flowers, delicate blades of grass, a single, shining leaf.

Could you declare a time-out later today, and take a half-hour to soak up God's creation, great and small? Pick a flower. Take a walk. Feel the snow or sun on your face. Listen to the whispering wind. Give yourself time to hear the Creator's voice.

PRAYER: Thank You, Father, for Your life-giving hand. Help me to open my eyes, and recognize Your fingerprints all around me.

No need to pretend

READ I CORINTHIANS 12:12-27.
"There should be no division in the body, but . . .
the members should have the same care for one
another." I Corinthians 12:25

"Grandma, can I wear those high heels? I'm
playing dress-up!"

I looked at five-year-old Lauren and stifled a
laugh. Large brown eyes entreated me under
the faded brim of a green thrift store hat.
Small hands crushed the trailing ends of a
purple velvet stole to her chest. Toes wiggled
in anticipation of the final touch: Grandma's
high heels.

For all of that rainy afternoon Lauren wob-
bled around the house in her finery, high heels
slapping our wooden kitchen floor in uneven
staccato. Near dinner time, hungry and weary

of pretend, she pulled the hat from her head, dumped the stole unceremoniously on top of it, and kicked off the heels.

"Grandma, I'm so glad I'm me!" she exclaimed, throwing herself on the couch. I hugged her, echoing her delight in who she was.

Are you a dress-up parent? Have you wrapped yourself in deceptive garments of apparent competency? Does a wide-brimmed hat of hollow serenity hide the pain in your eyes? Do you walk tall in public, but stagger with fatigue when you're alone?

Do you, like Lauren, long to shed pretense? Is it time to toss your happy face mask aside? The safest place to practice that kind of honesty is in your church. Its people have also known pain, and they will understand. Reach out today, and share what's really going on at home.

PRAYER: Forgive me, Lord, for pretending to be what I am not. Help me this day to tell one person how I actually feel.

God's comforting presence

∽

READ PSALM 25:16-22.
"I am lonely and afflicted . . . bring me out of my distresses." Psalm 25:16b,17

And your husband?" I asked a caregiver I hadn't seen in several years, and whose husband had Alzheimer's disease. "How is he doing?"

"He died eight months ago," she said softly. "He went downhill so fast. . . . I was with him at the end." Tears flooded her eyes and she looked away. "It seems like yesterday. . . . I'm still dealing with it," she explained.

Caregiving begins because one person needs help from another. Your loved one may be an elderly parent or parent-in-law, an adult brother or sister, or perhaps a child. It may even be one of the most difficult challenges of all—looking after a beloved husband or wife.

Besides the plain hard work of daily responsibility for another person, the emotional pain of spousal caregiving is like no other. "We were so bonded after thirty-three years of marriage," my friend continued. "He changed so much, I couldn't make him well, and I felt so helpless and sad. I'm trying to put my life back together, but there's such a void. . . ."

"I am lonely and afflicted," the psalmist cries in today's reading. "The troubles of my heart are enlarged." Perhaps you're caring for your wife or husband, and you're saying "Yes, Lord, that's exactly how I feel." God hears your cry. He feels your tears. As He hung on the cruel cross, His torturous separation and loneliness became our bridge to the Father. He understands your affliction, your aching heart. Though you cannot see Him, He walks close beside you through this dark and shadowed valley.

PRAYER: I have never known such pain before, Father. Thank You for Your comforting presence through this endless night.

How's your spiritual barometer?

—— ∞ ——

READ PSALM 40:1-5.
*"How blessed is the man who has made the
Lord his trust." Psalm 40:4a*

A fork clattered onto a plate and Betty, the
owner of a Christian group home, smiled
knowingly.

"Esther," she asked gently, circling the nod-
ding woman's hand with her own, "do you
think it's about time for bed?"

"I guess so," the old woman laughed. "I'm
falling asleep."

Betty unlocked the wheelchair braces and
turned it toward her patient's room. "Shall we
read a little from the Bible, Esther?"

"Oh, yes, I'd like that." A few minutes later
her eyes closed again, soothed by the now
familiar and comforting rhythm of Scripture.

Since moving into the group home eighteen months before, Esther's almost ninety-year-old body had steadily declined. But her spiritual growth, in the midst of marked physical deterioration, soon became the greatest surprise and joy of Betty's group home ministry.

Reserved about spiritual things, Esther soon asked Betty to read to her from the Bible in her room. At first reluctant to pray except at meals, before long she extended her hands to Betty, wanting her to pray for a concern. As the end of her life neared, she drew visibly closer to God.

Though you may not run a group home, how's your own spiritual barometer? Do you reassure and encourage the people you care for each day? Take a moment right now, and ask God to show how you can make Him more immediate and real to those you work and live with.

PRAYER: Today Lord, please help me to be more sensitive to spiritual needs, and thankful for the tiniest growth.

One you can count on

⸺ ∽ ⸺

READ ISAIAH 53:1-7.
*"He was despised and forsaken of men, a man
of sorrows, and acquainted with grief."*
Isaiah 53:3a

No matter who it is you're taking care of,
sooner or later someone lets you down.
Perhaps, more than anything in the world, you
need a breather from the relentless pressure of
your husband's depression. But the night
before your getaway your brother-in-law calls
to say he won't be able to come—he forgot
about an all-day class. Or maybe you've spent
weeks planning a surprise birthday party for a
physically challenged child, and six of your ten
guests don't show up.

    Is your heart aching because the people you
counted on ran the other way? Do relatives

know your situation well, yet rarely call or stop by? Did too many fair-weather friends disappear when your life's surface got choppy?

Today's Isaiah passage remains one of the great treasures of the Old Testament. In it the Spirit of the living God leads the prophet to describe the suffering servant, Jesus the Messiah. In verse after verse he tells of Christ's own grief and sorrow as men despised and abandoned Him.

Have family or friends let you down? Take a moment to reread this passage, and let it lead you alongside the living Lord. Reach for His nail-scarred hand. Allow Him to be your dearest companion down the anguished path of disillusionment and neglect.

PRAYER: Lord, I thought so many would understand and help, especially (add your own words). Teach me to forgive, as You forgave.

We're in this together

⸿

READ EPHESIANS 4:20-25.
"We are members of one another."
Ephesians 4:25b

L ast night Ned finished his sixth business trip
in a month," his wife explained. "When he
first walked in it was almost as if his eyes
were asking, 'Who're you?' I couldn't believe it!"

"He's been out of town six times?" her friend
asked.

"Six, with one more before the month ends.
And when he is home he's doing paper work
most of the time. I know how important his job
is, but he never stops. It's almost as if it's the
most important thing in his life. . . ."

Workaholism clogs the pores of every relationship, replacing spontaneity and joy with
fear and distrust. Family neglect inevitably
results. Rarely intended, seldom acknowl-

edged, it is always destructive.

How's your own family doing? Have you taken a good look at those you live with lately? Is there an absent father . . . or mother? How long since all of you enjoyed some time together? Or like Ned, has someone in your family allowed a work addiction to alienate those he or she loves most?

Could it be time to make some changes in your house? ".Therefore, laying aside falsehood," today's Scripture teaches, "speak truth, each one of you, with his neighbor, for we are members of one another." Ask, and God will enable you to lovingly confront. He desires truth for every member of your family, for He has made you members of one another.

PRAYER: Father, I see things in my family that need changing. Show me the time and place to share with (add your own words) what I see going on. And please Lord, give me kind and gentle words.

The darkness won't last forever

⸻

READ PSALM 30.
"Weeping may last for the night, but a shout of joy comes in the morning." Psalm 30:5b

What are you looking at, Chris?" Grandfather studied the five-year-old boy perched cross-legged in the twilight, his back pressed against a stuccoed wall still warm from the desert heat.

"I'm just listening to the night," the husky child whispered.

Have you noticed how darkness varies, how different one night can be from another? Some wrap you in a friendly hug, like Christopher's summer evening. Others whistle down the corridor of a changing season, weakening autumn's grasp with blowing fury. Many bring weeping skies, restoring parched soil. Not a few immobilize long midnights with crippling snow.

Nights spent caring for a sick child can seem to never end. During those exhausting hours your little one may summon you to the bedside, wincing in pain, hoping for sleep that will not come.

Is your son or daughter sick? If so, take time to examine the nights of your nursing vigil. As illness travels its course, your care will also change. Some nights will be summer soft, when you and your child enjoy safe harbor. Then suddenly the unknown may strike, terrifying you with the icy winds of change. But God has promised no night will last forever. Always, laughing in the face of fear, He brings the dawn. And with it, His strength and joy.

PRAYER: *Give me eyes to see Your presence during illness, Lord. Help me to glimpse dawn beyond the darkest night.*

Blessings in disguise

———— ∞ ————

READ ISAIAH 55:8-12.
"'My thoughts are not your thoughts, neither are your ways My ways,' declares the Lord."
Isaiah 55:8

Trick or treat!"
I seized a basket of wrapped carmel candy, unlocked the door, and heard muffled giggles. On the porch, gentle candlelight from our smiling pumpkin flickered over two masked rabbits. In the darkness behind them a parental sentry waved to me in silence.

"Trick or treat!" they shouted again.

As I dropped candies into each outstretched bag, the murmured thanks identified our visitors. Though I didn't see them often, I recognized the twins from two streets away. In a flash they were on their way, cotton-stuffed bunny ears flopping in the cold October wind.

I thought of them the next morning while I picked candy wrappers from the street and dumped the shriveling pumpkin into the trash. Though I hardly believed rabbits had stopped by for a friendly visit last night, working past their disguises had taken time.

As with those costumed children, I am equally slow to recognize God's hidden blessings. "How can I be thankful for three little boys with chicken pox?" I'll grumble. "Or for Dad's missing false teeth?" Fortunately, God's thoughts are not my thoughts, nor His ways mine. Take a look at your day. Can you spot a disguise that may conceal one of God's choice blessings for your life?

PRAYER: Lord, help me to look past first impressions. Slow me down, so I may recognize Your blessings in disguise.

Peace in place of panic

⸙

READ PHILIPPIANS 4:4-9.
"And the peace of God, which surpasses all comprehension, shall guard your hearts and your minds in Christ Jesus." Philippians 4:7

Could you put Keri and Joe on the Prayer Chain?"

"You bet. How shall we word it?"

"They're bringing the new baby home next Tuesday. Their first one died of Sudden Infant Death Syndrome two years ago."

"We'll start praying immediately."

"Thanks so much, and . . . could you also include her mother? She's helping them for two weeks, and she's so apprehensive."

From the world's point of view this couple had plenty to worry about. Bringing any new baby home demands faith, a commodity Keri and Joe would need in mega-doses. But in today's Bible reading God has provided a sure antidote to the world's viewpoint.

Perhaps you've recently had disturbing or frightening news about a relative's health, or maybe your own. Our Prayer Chain delighted to pray for Keri, Joe, their baby, her mother, and their family. We wrapped them by name in the peace of God which surpasses all comprehension. We prayed the for Holy Spirit to guard their hearts and their minds in Christ Jesus.

What is your worst fear today? Look straight at it; then banish its power with the Word of God. Enfold that fear, and your own mind and heart, with Christ's boundless peace.

PRAYER: Oh Lord, sometimes my fears wither all hope, especially when I think of (add your own words). Flood me with Your peace that stretches far beyond my understanding.

An approving Father

⚭

READ I CORINTHIANS 4:1-5.
"Then each man's praise will come to him from God." *I Corinthians 4:5b*

M y parents never allowed me to feel that I
was special," recalls a famous movie star.
"I wish they would have. I wanted my father's
approval more than anything in the world. I
worked so hard to get it, but I never did. I
always had to prove my worth."

You're probably not an actress, but perhaps
this woman's words could be your own. Tragic
as her feelings were, at least she didn't have to
deal with them week after week. She had lost
her parents years ago. But you may have to
interact on a regular basis with a silent, criti-
cal relative impossible to please.

Today's Scripture may not fill the longing

void within you. A part of who you are may for-ever wait for your relative's praise, for the unrestrained words of affirmation and pleasure he or she never says. For reasons complex and unknown, that person cannot or will not cele-brate the one-of-a-kind person named You.

But there is Someone who does, whose praise is lavish, unmeasured, and never ends. Next time you're with that relative, turn your ear away from the habit of straining to catch words that do not come, may never come. By all means, continue to be gentle and loving.

But as you do, train yourself to listen for the Holy Spirit's voice within your soul. He is well pleased, delighted, honored by your life. He sees, He knows, He understands. And He praises You with endless love.

PRAYER: *There is an empty place within me Lord, and I lift up longing hands. Satis-fy my hungry heart with You alone.*

Seasons

━━━━━━━━━━ ∞ ━━━━━━━━━━

READ I CORINTHIANS 2:6-10.
"Things which eye has not seen and ear has not heard . . . God has prepared for those who love Him." I Corinthians 2:9

This morning we took an early walk through one of our rambling city parks. October's golden wash shimmered over cobalt sky, amber leaves, and emerald grass. Above trim flower beds orange and yellow marigolds bumped shoulders, bowing low in a lavish, final curtain call.

We strode ahead, our breath frosty despite the sun, savoring the silent, seasonal chorus surrounding us. "Enjoy each moment," we seemed to hear. "Soon enough it will end." The lyrics were right, of course. Brevity deepens October's beauty, ever shadowed by cold

November. That day we heeded the unspoken message and concentrated on our present, rebuking mournful thoughts of approaching winter.

Autumn traces a pattern for all of the varied ways we care. Contentment and quiet joys burnish its today, but loss, loneliness, and separation often haunt its tomorrow. Like shining October, caring seasons too will end. And though we may embrace November's release, we may also look back and weep.

For Christians, God's transcendent power embraces both seasons. Verse nine of today's Bible passage proclaims the glorious mysteries God has prepared for those who love Him. Have tears, regrets, and sorrow numbed your bleak November? From those same moments will emerge a fresh creation, His endless October.

PRAYER: *Thank You, Lord, that the world's endings unwrap Your beginnings. Graft in my fearful heart the reality of Your love.*

Love is gracious

―――――――――― ∞ ――――――――――

READ I CORINTHIANS 13:1-13.
"If I speak with the tongues of men and of
angels, but do not have love, I have become a
noisy gong or a clanging cymbal."
I Corinthians 13:1

D o you like french fries too?" Jim asked.
Our cardiac support group had met for
over a year, but I'd never seen his eyes so
bright.

"They were my staff of life," I laughed, "until
they got out of hand."

"We went out to dinner last night," he continued, his tone almost reverent. "I ordered
chopped steak and french fries and ate every
bite!"

"Did you say anything?" I joked with his

116

wife, remembering her husband's near-fatal heart attack.

"Not one word! she laughed. "After thirty-six years of marriage you learn when to speak up, and when to stay quiet!"

She could have quoted statistics about saturated fats. She might have pouted or grown angry, ruining his feast. But she loved her husband and understood him well—including his passion for french fries. She also knew that he would mentally dine on last night's repast through long months of salads and fish.

Has someone in your life strayed too often from the food guide pyramid? Would his or her occasional outbursts flunk the good manners test? Were Mom's false teeth sitting in the soft drink coaster your guest reached for? Does any of it really matter? Take time to slowly reread today's beautiful Scripture passage. Then pray that for this one day your relationships may be saturated with accepting love.

PRAYER: *Father, I want to reflect Your love in all I do today. Help me to remember that love often means saying nothing.*

Slowing the "rat race"

∞

READ GENESIS 2:1-3.
"And He rested on the seventh day from all His work which He had done." Genesis 2:2b

Do you remember the last time you wandered through a pet store? You passed cages of wrestling puppies, sleeping kittens, and preening parakeets. Maybe you found a section reserved for hamsters, those small tan animals with bright eyes, tiny ears, and an obsession with running.

During my child-raising years I thought often of our family's long-gone hamster. Twenty-four hours a day he did one of three things: nibbled seeds and grain, snoozed under shredded newspapers, or whizzed around and around and around on a metal wheel.

As I dashed from John's Little League game

to Matt's, fixed four sack lunches after dinner, then ironed a uniform so I could get up at five and do it all over again, I felt exactly like that racing hamster.

One day I decided to end my mad dash. At my most efficient, I only kept even with the demand. And what was it all for? During the next month I reread the Creation story each night, concentrating on the Genesis verses. Even our mighty Lord, after forming the world, allowed Himself to rest.

As mine once did, does your life resemble a hamster on a wheel? Would you get so terribly behind if you allowed yourself one day off, one day when you did only the absolute essentials? Could you try it this week? Right now, ask God to help you bless every seventh day, sanctify it, and receive His healthy provision of weekly rest from your endless work.

PRAYER: *It's hard to let go Lord, but Your example makes it so much easier. Show me how to set apart the seventh day, as You did.*

Words to live by

―――――― ∞ ――――――

READ II TIMOTHY 3:14-17.
"All Scripture is inspired by God and profitable for teaching, for reproof, for correction, for training in righteousness." II Timothy 3:16

"Seventy-nine degrees," flashed the sign as I completed my left turn.

"11:24 a.m.," it blinked while I picked up speed.

"Wednesday, May 3," it reminded me as I drove past.

I timed my exits from our street by that electronic wonder. My eyes sought it out, eager for confirmation of date, time, and more.

Then one day it disappeared, accompanied by a cardboard "For Rent or Lease" sign taped to the store window behind it. Only a gaping hole in the lawn remained, a reminder of the sturdy pole that once supported the friendly sign. Though months have passed, my eyes still search for its announcements. I took it for granted, assuming it would always be there. Now it's gone. I miss it, and the continuity it lent to my daily errands.

The Bible is a little like that sign indicator. It never forces itself upon the reader, but waits patiently to be read. And then its encouragement, information, comfort, counsel, and inspiration stabilize and transform every moment of the reader's day.

What are your days like? Is daily Bible reading a part of them? Or are you too busy to take time, too exhausted to stay awake, too close to the brink of desperation? Slowly reread today's verses, and encounter once again the matchless, life-giving power of Scripture.

PRAYER: Thank You, Lord, for the incomparable gift of Your Word. Help me to make its study the highest priority of my life.

Establishing reasonable limits

❦

READ JAMES 3:13-18.
*"The wisdom from above is first pure, then
peaceable, gentle, reasonable, full of mercy and
good fruits, unwavering, without hypocrisy."*
James 3:17

When my husband's invalid mother came
to live with us, my naive expectations
soon crumbled under caregiving's realities. It'll
be a piece of cake! I'd thought. I'll simply get
up as early, move as fast, plan as well, and
stay up as late as the situation demanded.

My life would continue as before: Vacation
Bible School, dinner with friends, Bible study,
writing, Prayer Chain link, early morning walks,
relaxed Sunday afternoons, and more. I convinced myself that I could neatly slip caregiving
into the few remaining spaces of each day.

That theory exploded the day I fell sound asleep in church for the first time in my life, and realized something had to give. Dead ahead loomed a crossroads: simplify my schedule or collapse under its weight.

Are you facing a similar change point in your life? Does an avalanche of yesterday's commitments threaten to bury today's reality? Do you cry easily? Lash out at those you love with words you loathe? Drag yourself into bed praying tomorrow never comes?

Join hands with overcommitted people around the world who have reduced their obligations. Ask God to bathe you with His wisdom, to make clear what duties you must ask to be excused from. Let Him reveal what has become a burden, and what to do about it. Then obey the Holy Spirit's voice. Dial the phone and say, "Thank you, but I can't right now."

PRAYER: Lord, I've taken on too much, especially (add your words). Please give me strength to make that phone call—today.

Letting hope shine through

―――――― ∞ ――――――

READ I PETER 3:13-15.
"Always being ready to . . . give an account
for the hope that is in you. . . ." *I Peter 3:15*

My friend Judy glimpsed a white-haired woman helping her partially paralyzed husband shuffle his way up the stone steps into church.

She moved quickly alongside them and grasped the man's other arm. Two minutes later and short of breath, he lowered himself into a polished pew. "Thanks," he wheezed, smiling up at her.

With a few minutes remaining before the service, Judy and the elderly woman walked outside again.

"Lavina," my friend asked. "How do you do it every Sunday?"

"I don't—dear, the Lord does," she said gently.

"How do you mean?"

"Whenever we're tempted to give up on church, Jesus takes over and gives us strength to get here. He's the one keeps us going."

Tears misted Judy's eyes several times during that Sunday worship service. All through the week, whenever she felt discouraged she drew strength from the example of Lavina and her husband.

Caregivers often search for help among family and friends, not recognizing the power of their own witness. Is Jesus Christ the one who keeps you going? Be ready, like Lavina, to give an account of that hope within you. God will use your own testimony, told with gentleness and reverence, to build up other believers in ways you never dreamed.

PRAYER: Thank You, Lord, for my hope that comes from You. Help me to boldly tell all who ask that You alone are its reason.

Worship His majesty

⌘

READ PSALM 145:1-7.
*"Every day I will bless Thee, and I will praise
Thy name forever and ever." Psalm 145:2*

Late one summer afternoon I drove up a mile-
high mountain, snaking my way along the
winding highway. An hour later, sunset crept
over the darkening peaks. Not satisfied with
furtive glances at the unfolding panorama, I
pulled off the highway to a graveled scenic
turnout.

In the valley below me, crimson, lavender,
and gold illumined a carpet of rippling clouds.
Above their cotton softness towered the cobalt,
sentinel peaks of the mountain range. The
sun's last rays, reluctant to leave, shimmered
over all in gilded coral and lavender.

I stood alone for many moments, absorbing
the luminous beauty that stretched to the

horizon. I desired no statistics of cloud depth, density, or geologic mountain age. The pulsing wonder of the setting supplied all I could hope to know, mirroring the image of the Creator's hand. In silence I soaked it in, worshiping with body, mind, and spirit. Since that day its summoned memory has many times brought quiet and fresh perspective to my troubled soul.

Think back to the most beautiful scene in your own memory—perhaps a glassy lake in early morning, or mighty waves crashing against steep granite cliffs. Close your eyes, and allow yourself to see, smell, and hear it once again. For a moment forget yourself and your vigils of care. Worship your Creator God. Bathe your spirit in the wonder of His presence.

PRAYER: One generation shall praise Your works to another, O Lord. I will praise Your name forever and ever.

What lurks beneath the surface?

<hr>

READ MARK 4:21-23.
"For nothing is hidden, except to be revealed."
Mark 4:22a

For four days heavy white flakes blanketed everything in sight with eighteen inches of snow. Our street buzzed with the muffled sounds of snowblowers and the scrape of shovels against frozen asphalt.

On the surface the landscape radiated purity, but underneath skulked another story. Tired motors had rocketed thick black oil into snowbanks. Antifreeze and gasoline had chewed ugly craters through the frozen frosting. Four days later the city snowplow finally powered through our neighborhood. When it turned the corner, six foot piles of clean snow camouflaged those crumbling stains.

As new piles of snow shrouded the globs of grease, Sam hid the pain of his father's drunken rages far below his life's surface. No one must ever know why he always ate alone—that while he was growing up his father battered his son's head with a toaster at almost every meal.

As with the plow's frozen residue, in time God melted the counterfeit surface of Sam's life. Twenty-eight years later he sobbed forth his secret betrayal and pain. And in that brutal honesty the seeds of forgiveness, understanding, and healing at last took root.

Does the make-believe surface of your life cover a disfiguring stain? Why not make this the day you confess it to the Lord? Pour out your heart to Him; then ask the Holy Spirit to lead you to the counsel you may need. Reveal your secret, and He will cleanse you from the inside out.

PRAYER: *Forgive me, Lord, for burying the truth. Help me to expose the ugly parts of my life to Your transforming light.*

No small achievements

⚉

READ PSALM 98.
"His right hand and His holy arm have gained
the victory for Him." Psalm 98:1b

Mom, look!"
His mother turned from the sink, tired
eyes seeking her thirteen-year-old son's wheelchair. He smiled up at her, waiting.

Then his strangely clean plate drew her eyes
as a magnet attracts iron. "Jimmy!" she
gasped. "What happened to your dinner?"

"I ate it!"

"But . . . how?" Use of his arms and legs had
ended five years ago, when he dove off a bridge
into shallow water, severing his spinal cord.

"I propped up my arms, Mom, like this . . ."
He grasped a spoon with both hands and tipped
his head under it, mouth wide open.

Psalm 98 celebrates the Lord's mighty victory,

won by His power and holiness. Jimmy pro-
claimed another kind of conquest, achieved by
raw determination and courage. Both call for
joyful shouts and glad praises.

You became a caregiver because someone
you love needed help. Yet that person still
yearns for a normal life, still battles against
disease and helplessness. And occasionally,
like a silver salmon battling her way upstream,
a small achievement breaks through the strong
current of your loved one's affliction. Could
you make this the day you both celebrate one
of those tiny triumphs he thought nobody
noticed?

**PRAYER: Father, thank You for the gar-
ments of victory. May I always remember
that You send them in many sizes.**

Facing the future by looking back

⚯

READ PSALM 89:1-11.
"To all generations I will make known Thy faithfulness. . . ." Psalm 89:1b

Karyn snuggled onto the couch, set a mug of peppermint tea close by, placed the brand-new calendar on her lap, and opened it to January. She enjoyed this New Year's Day ritual, the annual transfer of birthday and anniversary dates from the old year to the new.

An hour later she finished, picked up both calendars, and headed for the wastebasket. But for the first time in her memory she didn't want to let the old one go. Its worn pages detailed one of the hardest years she'd ever known—the year a hunting accident paralyzed her husband from the waist down. Though his therapy, medicines, and bulky equipment compressed every part of her life, with God's help they'd made it through.

Karyn glanced at the new calendar's clean, blank squares. What might the next twelve months hold? Could she manage a full-time job? Would she and Jim ever again have a normal life together? She studied the bright January picture of a snow-covered bridge, and reread the Scripture beneath it: "To all generations I will make known Thy faithfulness."

Your tomorrow, like Karyn's, is also unknown. But above you both, God's faithfulness shines like the morning star. Just for a moment close your eyes, and journey back through the milestones and challenges of the past year. Did God walk with you each step of the way? Did He supply each day's needs? Does He ever change? Now consciously let go of every whisper of fear, and slip your hand in His.

PRAYER: Lord, thank You for Your faithfulness through the past year. I trust You to unfold the page of each new day.

Don't give up

⤫

READ PSALM 147:1-5.
"He heals the brokenhearted." Psalm 147:3a

L aura and I could never seem to get along,"
admitted a young girl's aunt.

"Do you know why?" asked a support group
member.

"It began after her mother died, when we
brought her to live with us," she explained, her
voice catching. "She always seemed angry,
especially at me. I understood, but I still
hoped. . . ."

"The past year must have been really hard
for both of you."

"It has been. I almost dreaded her birthday
last week."

"How did it go?"

"When I set the cake in front of her I hugged
her and said, 'We love you, Laura.' I expected

her to pull away. But I couldn't believe what happened. She started to cry, right there with thirteen candles burning and all of us singing 'Happy Birthday'!"

"Did she say anything?"

She paused, brushing away tears. "Yes— after a minute or two she hugged me again and said, 'I love you, too.' It was as if those four words began to wash away all the pain we'd both felt for so long."

Have you almost given up on a situation in your own family? Did you know there is nothing impossible with God, nothing He cannot heal? Confess your own unforgiveness, and let Him mend your broken heart.

PRAYER: Father, You understand the pain I've carried for so long. I want to be free of it, Lord. Grant me the grace to forgive those who have hurt me, that I may receive Your healing.

The only opinion that counts

READ I SAMUEL 16:1-13.
"Man looks at the outward appearance, but the Lord looks at the heart." I Samuel 16:7

"Did you have a good holiday?" I asked a caregiving friend.

"It was wild," she replied, shaking her head. "Two days before Christmas Dad was standing by their kitchen sink, stark naked, muttering about fixing something. Mom called me after he threw a vacuum cleaner attachment at her. She was really scared."

Several times a week my friend drove her parents to appointments, and carted dinners to their apartment. Every day she phoned them. Now she must grapple with the reality that her father might harm her mother.

"We had to place him in a nursing home for

evaluation, and he may never be able to live with Mom again. The agonizing part is deciding where he would go. The family thinks it's a great idea for him to live with Bob and me. But I just can't take care of Mom, Bob's mother, and have Dad with us all at the same time. We've got to have a quiet place to restore our own energy. But everyone else has other ideas for us . . . it's so hard."

Have you reached a fork in your own care-giving road? Are friends and family insisting you do something while your heart cries out "I can't!"? Today's Scripture explains that man sees only the outward things. You will make wiser decisions by seeking counsel from professionals, family, and friends. But the Lord alone knows your heart, your strengths, your limitations. Listen, that you may hear His gentle voice above all the others.

PRAYER: Thank You for creating me, Lord. Thank You for seeing the inward things, and for understanding the cries of my heart.

Preparing for
tomorrow—today

READ JOHN 13:1-5.
"[Jesus] . . . rose from supper, and laid aside
His garments; and taking a towel, He girded
Himself about." John 13:4

"Prepare now for winter!" urged a cheerful
red and white banner in front of the gas
station.

"Don't wait—let us winterize your car!" it
concluded, flapping wildly in the late October
wind. The sign offered a timely reminder to
prepare for winter: check heater hoses, replace
windshield wipers, change to lighter weight oil,
tune the engine.

In a sense, every parent's routine needs year-
round winterizing. Washing machines will mal-
function at the worst time. Unannounced family or friends will tax the most flexible routine.

And the unthinkable does happen: a cold, flu, or minor emergency will occasionally sideline the most vigorous mom or dad.

Today's revered introductory verses from John's gospel reveal an often overlooked scriptural nugget. Loving His disciples, desiring to model for the last time their servant-calling, Jesus got up from supper to wash their feet. But notice what He did first; he took a towel and wrapped it around Himself. Jesus prepared Himself for the task ahead.

What future parenting challenges may confront you? Follow the Lord's example—think about them now. Ask Him to guide you to exactly the information, supports, and spiritual resources you may need in the years ahead. He has gone before, and will walk with you each step of the way.

PRAYER: *Lord, I have so much to do today it's hard to think of tomorrow. Show me what I can do now, that I may be prepared.*

Never beyond His reach

———————— ∞ ————————

READ DEUTERONOMY 33:26-29.
". . . And underneath are the everlasting arms."
Deuteronomy 33:27

My sister and I tiptoed into her daughter's corner of the Intensive Care Unit. Above her left shoulder a greenish-yellow monitor belched endless diagrams of every heartbeat.

I cupped my hand over Bonnie's, careful not to jiggle the needle taped to the back of her pale hand. Her cold fingers moved slightly against mine and I pulled the yellow flannel blanket over them.

"Some people will do anything to get out of school," I joked.

She smiled, worried eyes searching for her mother.

A few moments later I said good-bye and

returned to the wide hall crisscrossed by green-clad nurses who somehow still managed to smile. My sister soon joined me, having used up her allotted five minutes of each hour with Bonnie.

"I feel as if this isn't happening," she told me, steadying her trembling mouth. "It's as if I'm floating."

That night I thought about her words. "Float: to be or cause to be suspended, unsupported in space," said my dictionary. "And underneath," replied my Bible, " are the everlasting arms." Does fear shadow this day for you? Has uncertainty shaken your trusted foundations? Make the eternal God your dwelling place, remembering that no accident, no technology, no hospital bed—*nothing* can separate you from His love.

PRAYER: Lord, You know that sometimes I am afraid, especially when I think of (add your own words). Thank You that I can never move beyond Your loving, outstretched arms.

Pure light for the darkest night

⊗

READ EXODUS 15:1-13.
"Who is like Thee, majestic in holiness, awesome in praises . . . ?" Exodus 15:11

"The medicine should help . . . and I'll come right back," I promised. Guided by the pale glow of our son's night light, I tiptoed to the door and eased it shut.

I'd slipped from my bed to go into his room four times during that long, mid-December night. Pneumonia had invaded his young body in early December, leaving him with a dry, tight cough that reverberated through three walls.

But instead of rushing back to bed I wandered down the dark hall, fatigue screaming from the muscles of my back, despair clogging my mind. Would the night ever end? When

would the medicine take effect? Would I ever
be rested? I stopped in the entry hall, not sure
what I wanted or why I was there. On impulse I
moved to the manger scene, searched out the
five-watt bulb inside the crude wooden stable,
and twisted it on.

Joseph stood tall, surrounded by thirty-
year-old straw. Across from him knelt Mary,
her graceful hands clasped in wonder. Between
them smiled the tiny Christ child, God's gift of
hope. In the predawn darkness I knelt before
it, releasing my anguish.

Right now, the same Christ who brought
light to a darkened world yearns to bathe your
spirit in the radiance of His love. Because He
came, you can continue. Because He lives,
your battle is already won.

**PRAYER: Father, some nights seem murky
and endless. Help me to see Your love
beaming light into my blackest midnight.**

Alone, but not abandoned

———— ∞ ————

READ PROVERBS 30:4, 5.
"He is a shield to those who take refuge in Him." Proverbs 30:5b

I stirred my morning coffee and peered out at the thick darkness. Suddenly the phone's shrill ring jarred my senses, gripping my heart with fear. Had something happened to one of the children?

They were fine, but my caregiving friend, three states away, wasn't. "I'm sorry to call at this hour," she began, her voice tight with coiled desperation. "I've been at the hospital all night with Jim. . . ."

"What's happened?"

"The cancer's spread to his brain. We were so certain the surgery got it all." Her voice broke, weighting the line with silence. "Jim doesn't know me anymore. It's as if he disappeared overnight. We've always done everything together, and now I've lost him!" She stifled a sob.

Though three months would pass before her husband's physical death, she had indeed lost him in every other sense. Terrified, she felt utterly abandoned. There was only one way I could help: listen to her. In the months that followed she grew stronger, and by phone and letter we explored God's promises to those who are alone. Today's verses from Proverbs provided a sturdy support her wilting spirit could lean against.

Perhaps you, like my grieving friend, care for a loved one who no longer knows you. Would you reach out in faith? Sometime today, read a psalm, or another Bible passage. Listen for God's voice, talk to Him. He waits for you, longing to become your comfort, your shield, your friend.

PRAYER: *Father, my life has turned inside out and I feel so alone. Speak to me now as I take refuge Your Word.*

Our quake-proof foundation

⚉

READ II SAMUEL 22:29-34.
"And who is a rock, besides our God?"
II Samuel 22:32b

During my sixteenth summer, a warm
August evening erupted into a nightmare.
After a leisurely salad dinner on the patio my
family went upstairs. While we visited together
the floor suddenly convulsed, making our
house shake and moan like a wounded animal.
Crying, my mother, sister and I clung to each
other in the middle of the room.

"Earthquake!" shouted my father. "Get
under the doorways!"

We obeyed, and for countless seconds that
seemed to stretch to eternity, I huddled against
the doorjamb. Our home's sturdy floors swayed
like a wooden ocean as I listened to strange

snapping noises inside the roof and walls. Abruptly, the cataclysm ended as silently as it had begun.

After one of my little boys was diagnosed with leukemia, I thought back to that terrifying experience many times. Just hearing the name of his illness hurled shock waves through every facet of my life. But the hardest part became my fear that a medical crisis, like that long ago earthquake, would strike my son and find me unprepared.

In the four months before Christopher's death, I learned that only God could be my foundation, my rock. It was impossible to prepare myself for every future what-if, every possible unknown. Like the timbers of our childhood home, my knowledge—and yours—has limits of endurance and ability. God's power always anchors the world's wisdom.

PRAYER: Thank You, Father, for my ministry of caring. Teach me to be wise, to acquaint myself with what I should know. Then help me to let that go, Lord, and trust in You, my cornerstone.

Reach out and touch . . .

———— ∽ ————

READ I THESSALONIANS 5:8-11.
"Therefore encourage one another, and build up one another. . . ." I Thessalonians 5:11

We're responsible to a higher Power!" read the advertising slogan of a national car rental agency. True or not, it was catchy. I still remember it many years later.

When I was a single mother, I tried hard to give care in the same spirit. No one witnessed ninety per cent of what I did for my small children. I could easily have reused dirty sheets or ignored meals or kept the shades drawn day and night. Who would know?

But I'd invited the Lord to walk beside me through it all, and He did. Like the car rental agency, I too was responsible to a Higher Power. His name was the Lord Jesus Christ, and as a single Mom I found my greatest encouragement from the reality of His presence.

But He understood my need for human assurance as well, and never failed to provide it when most needed. One friend called monthly, inviting all of us for a clean-out-the-refrigerator dinner. A retired neighbor stopped by regularly with a gleaming jar of her raspberry jam, "to sweeten your life as you're sweetening your family's," she'd explain.

Is there a single mom or dad among your friends? Could that person use a word of encouragement to brighten the often difficult days? Pray about it, listening for the name the Lord sends to your mind. Then reach out to that friend with the sacrament of encouragement.

PRAYER: Thank You for this new day, Lord. Please show me the person You desire to build up through me.

In His footsteps

∞

READ JOHN 1:1-13.
"He came to His own, and those who were His
own did not receive Him." John 1:11

I hated myself," wrote a woman struggling with
anger and resentment as she cared for her
controlling, ninety-three-year-old mother-in-law.
"I knew all I did was in vain, and that God hated
me for the way I felt. I knew I was a failure."

She and her husband had painted and car-
peted a vacant bedroom for his bitter mother,
helped her in and out of the tub, served her
accustomed three hot meals a day, and drove
her weekly to the doctor and hairdresser.
Because she complained about being alone,
they gave up all vacations and most of their
social life. Yet this caregiver was convinced she
had failed.

Reaching out to a loved one isn't like a military surgical strike. Needy people rarely move in alone; most drag knotted family relationships behind them. One person can't possibly unravel several or more decades of tangled family history. Yet many expect themselves to do so.

Are you in the midst of a no-win situation? Take time now to slowly reread today's Bible passage, concentrating on verse eleven. On the threshold of His earthly ministry Jesus encountered failure. He came to His own, the Jews, but they did not receive Him. He experienced everything you may feel: expectation, misunderstanding, disappointment, anger, frustration, embarrassment, and humiliating failure.

PRAYER: Thank You, Lord, that absolutely nothing I may go through is beyond Your experience. You have walked this road before me, and Your footsteps remain my guide.

Two-way communication

ↅ

READ I SAMUEL 3:1-10.
" . . .Speak, for Thy servant is listening."
I Samuel 3:10

I waxed this kitchen floor exactly one hour
ago, and now it's covered with muddy foot-
prints! Johnny, did you do this?"

Our four-year-old son bit his lower lip and
stared at the floor. "I guess so, Mom."

"But you know it's raining! I asked you to
take your boots off before you came in from the
backyard. Why didn't you?"

"Guess I wasn't listening."

That afternoon Johnny spent some creative
time on the kitchen floor learning about soapy
water and rags. But when he came in for supper late that afternoon he left his muddy boots
outside the back door.

Today's Scripture describes God's commissioning of the boy Samuel for his prophetic ministry. Unlike Johnny, Samuel avoided boot camp learning experiences because he was a finely tuned listener. "Speak," he told the Lord as he had been instructed, "for Thy servant is listening."

As a parent, are you practicing your most important survival skill—time alone with the Lord? Let Him refresh your spirit as you pray about one faith challenge after another. Just remember that essential as your prayers are, you also need to hear God speaking. By all means pour out your heart in prayer. Cry before the Lord, plead with Him, praise Him. But afterward, like Samuel, save some time for expectant silence.

PRAYER: *Father, thank You for Your readiness to hear my prayers. Teach me also to be quiet before You, that I may hear Your voice. Speak, for your servant is listening.*

Help is there for the asking

READ PSALM 73:21-26.
"With Thy counsel Thou wilt guide me."
Psalm 73:24b

In the closing days of December a wild winter storm churned over the Pacific Northwest, dumping two feet of snow. Then, typical for Eastern Washington, a warmer series of above-zero days followed, melting much of the snow by day, turning what remained into razored ice blocks by night.

Before long, frozen land mines littered the path of our early morning walk. Dirty mounds of stubborn old snow, perilous to walk on, clung to the soggy grass beneath. The storm's residue choked the ground, obstructing all growth and paralyzing our progress.

An adult recovering from illness may have to

contend with the mental clutter of similar debris. Painful remnants from childhood, long ago slights, perceived failures, simmering anger and neglect of every kind may clog his or her adjustment and recovery. As ancient snow chokes December's earth, refuse from the past often obstructs a relative's enjoyment of everyday life.

As ever when helping a loved one, take your suspicions first to the Lord. "With Thy counsel," He promises through the psalmist, "Thou wilt guide me." Seek that counsel. Might your relative need a helping hand from an outside source? A few sessions with a Christian counselor or insightful minister may be all that is needed. Has the time come to search out assistance for your relative, and indirectly for yourself?

PRAYER: *Father, help me to recognize past pain masquerading as anger or depression. Guide me with Your counsel, Lord.*

Divine perspective

∽

READ ISAIAH 52:6-10.
"How lovely . . . are the feet of him . . . who announces peace." Isaiah 52:7

I'll be going home soon, Mary . . . I want you to know."

The firm set of my mother-in-law's chin told me she meant it. I worked a pillow between her bony back and the padded recliner, wondering how to answer. "We'd be sorry to see you go. When would you be leaving?"

"As soon as I find my cane."

"Penny . . . uh, how would you manage that big house?" I didn't mention that the family had reluctantly agreed to sell her home three months ago.

"Why, the same as always!"

I knew that senile dementia caused her

confusion and memory loss, but I felt personally rejected, and after lunch retreated to my favorite hideaway along the Spokane River.

I plopped down on the coarse river sand and leaned against a warm granite boulder, listening. All around me hidden birds sang a counterpoint melody to the lapping rush of the silent, grey-blue river. A few feet from shore, tiny sprays of white lace foam veiled a cluster of glistening rocks.

An old board drifted by, then disappeared as I breathed in the smells of wet sand and sun-streaked willows. "Your caregiving ministry is like that piece of wood," the Spirit seemed to say. "Be patient. Its journey is also swift, and will soon be over." My rejection vanished like the floating board as God restored me with the peace of His perspective.

PRAYER: *Father, I feel so* (add your own words). *Lead me to a quiet place today, where I may bathe my spirit in Your peace.*

The one true source
of wisdom

∽

READ I CORINTHIANS 2:1-5.
*"That your faith should not rest on the wisdom
of men, but on the power of God."*
I Corinthians 2:5

"Try this book—the author's got degrees in medicine and in law."

Similar comments sprinkled the months after a friend's husband fell from a construction site scaffolding and broke his back. Hungry for information, Sue beat a path to the library and bookstore, reading everything friends suggested and a lot they didn't. Little by little her storehouse of knowledge grew.

She needed every bit of help she could get, and appreciated each suggestion. When the day came to bring Bud home, Sue had a good grasp of what to expect. Or so she thought,

until the newness wore off and she found herself wondering why he cried so often, and if
they could really afford to remodel the house
for a wheelchair, and why she couldn't sleep.

All of her scholarly how-to books failed to
remove so much as a speck of the resentment
Sue felt. Then one day she and Bud exchanged
bitter words. Fighting back tears, she opened
her Bible for help.

It didn't tell her what to do about Bud's specific situation, and it may not for yours.
Instead it focused on Sue, on the seething
anger and bitterness infecting her heart. Do
you long to blame someone else—anyone else—
for what is happening in your life? Have you
searched God's Word and confessed your sin?
He will lead you to the answers and actions
you may well need to take—but only when you
make Him first in your life.

**PRAYER: *Forgive me, Lord, for seeking wis-
dom everywhere but from You. Thank You
that Your timing and ways are perfect.***

The importance of rest

∽

READ PSALM 127.
"He gives to His beloved even in his sleep."
Psalm 127:2b

"These past two days," wrote a new mother,
"my highest priority has been to lie down
the minute I put Tony to bed. I've napped for
an hour or more, the kind of deep sleep I crave.
He's still awake a lot at night, and I've actually
been in sort of a slump. But since Tony came,
it's just so much harder to give myself permis-
sion to quit."

Twenty-four hours of every day Lori cares for
her two-week-old baby, knowing she must
return to work in less than two months, rested
or not. In her free time she used to write long
family letters, sew, attend an evening Bible
study, run several miles, and surprise her

husand with new recipes. Now she does well to get dressed, and feels guiltier by the minute.

For entirely different reasons maybe you, like this exhausted mother, also resist extra rest. Important new responsibilities have probably been heaped on your old ones. If you stop even for a nap, you're afraid they'll smother you like a collapsing sandpile. So you push yourself day after day, too close to your situation for any kind of perspective.

Do you put everyone else's needs before yours? Like Lori, perhaps you need encouragement to get that extra rest. Here it is: *because* you love your family, you *must* take care of yourself. Good health, beginning with rest, will shape you into the person God designed you to be.

PRAYER: I am tired, Lord, mostly because (add your own words). *Help me to make time today, or tonight, for extra sleep, Your restorative and gracious gift.*

God is on your side

READ ISAIAH 64:1-4.
"Neither has the eye seen a God besides Thee."
Isaiah 64:4b

Jessica's going to have the eye surgery next week."

"Can you manage taking care of her and your Mom, too?"

"I don't think so. I'm desperate for help, but I don't know where to start."

Perhaps you, like this single parent whose semi-invalid mother lives with her, have reached an impasse in the art of giving care. Changes are coming; you can feel it. Possibly something has happened, and a family member needs extra help from you or another relative. Maybe the gauge of your personal energy reserves registers empty, and you're searching for a way to refill the tank.

Have you been waiting for God, wondering what to do next? Slowly reread today's verses from Isaiah, and be encouraged. You serve a God who *works* on behalf of the one who waits for Him. That means He is way out in front of you, searching for solutions to your specific problem. He takes the initiative for you! He labors for you, far beyond anything you can imagine.

Today you may be burdened with wearisome problems. You may feel completely alone and deserted. But God has been occupied in solving your challenges long before you recognized them. Trust Him, talk to Him. Remember all He has already done for you, and take heart. Ask for His direction, and this very day He will meet you in the midst of your search.

PRAYER: *Thank You, Lord, for who You are! Thank You that You work for me even as I wait. Help me to see the solutions You send.*

Looking for an escape

∞

READ I CORINTHIANS 10:1-13.
*"No temptation has overtaken you but such as
is common to man."* I Corinthians 10:13a

The children of Israel experienced a glorious, one-on-one walk with God. He led them with a pillar of cloud by day and lit their path with a pillar of fire by night. He parted the swirling Red Sea and dried the land underneath so they could escape the brutal Egyptian army. Every morning He gave them manna to eat, and refreshed them with water from a rock.

In return the children of Israel lusted for Egyptian prostitutes and continually doubted God's power to provide for their circumstances. They grumbled, complained, and murmured against Him. Worst of all, they fashioned a golden calf from melted jewelry and worshiped it instead of God.

Has the dry desert of giving care played tricks with your memory and withered your soul? Are you weary of pressured schedules, endless lunches, and midnight cries for help? Has seductive Temptation visited you recently, not as a golden calf, but perhaps as a bottle hidden in the highest cupboard, or pills almost forgotten but not discarded, or a flickering screen that stifles every thought and conversation?

Whatever your personal temptation, God has seen it millions of times before. Even now He has set an escape hatch before you. All you need to do is open it. He longs to see you victorious over every circumstance in your life today. Never forget: He is faithful!

PRAYER: My temptation isn't a golden calf, Lord, but it is (supply your own words). Help me to recognize the way of escape you have provided for me, and to seize it now.

165

God's messengers
in disguise

―――――― ∞ ――――――

READ HEBREWS 13:1-6.
*"Do not neglect to show hospitality to strangers,
for by this some have entertained angels without knowing it." Hebrews 13:2*

H ow many words can she say?"
"Oh, not too many yet, but we can see her
trying." Donajeanne's smile hid her pain.

"None of her tests show what caused this,"
the pediatrician at Children's Hospital of Los
Angeles would soon explain. Thirty years later
Dianne still struggled with the same words
that baffled her at four.

One by one her grown brothers and sister
left home, leaving behind Dianne and her wide,
wondrous smile. Today she rides her bicycle,
listens to music, ice skates. She never stops
searching for ways to leap across the bottom-

less communication chasm that separates her from others.

What is it like to permanently share retirement with a dependent adult? "Everyone," Donajeanne smiles, "should receive the kind of love Dianne has given us."

God rarely wraps His choicest blessings in perfect paper. Maybe a gift arrived at your home a while back, a gift you didn't expect, aren't prepared for, and don't know how to manage. Maybe you're even afraid of it. Pray for grace to receive this strange present, to open it, and in time, to embrace it. An angel hides within, straight from the hand of God.

PRAYER: Father, I confess I never wanted **(name the person or circumstance you find most difficult to accept).** *Forgive me, Lord. Give me grace to love as You have loved, that I may welcome the angel You have wrapped inside this torn and damaged paper.*

Breaking the bonds
of the past

━━━━━━━━━━━━━ ⚭ ━━━━━━━━━━━━━

READ PHILIPPIANS 3:7-14.
*"But one thing I do: forgetting what lies behind
and reaching forward to what lies ahead."*
Philippians 3:13b

"When my Dad left home, it just tore up my world," cried a young husband. "I was nine . . . lost five pounds." His eyes clouded with pain.

He looked down and leaned against the washing machine. "Guess that's why I've never liked to rock the boat or confront things head on."

"I don't understand," his wife whispered.

"I thought Dad left because of something I'd done, that somehow I caused it. I was sure that if I could just be good enough, keep quiet enough, always try to . . ." he jerked the back of one hand across his eyes and looked away, ". . . maybe Mom and Dad would get back together again."

"But all that was thirty-five years ago. . . ."

For most of his life this father of three had dragged scarred anchors of memory behind him. In the weeks after this talk he and his wife took hold of the spiritual knife of prayer, and cut him loose from the crippling childhood ropes of fear and guilt.

What heavy anchors are you dragging through your life? Isn't it about time to cut them loose? Pray for strength to find a friend or group who will really listen, and understand, and help you break free. Some time today cut yourself a two-inch piece of rope, and put it in your pocket. During the day feel its raw, rough ends, and thank God for setting you free.

PRAYER: Lord Jesus, please cut me loose from the rusted anchors of (use your own words). I trust in Your power and in Your name alone.

Gaining perspective

READ PROVERBS 11:14.
"In abundance of counselors there is victory."
Proverbs 11:14b

B ut why not? Everyone on the swim team's going down early!"

"Honey, I'm sorry. Dad and I think you need to get a good night's sleep before the competition. Don't forget you had the flu last month."

"But I'm totally well now. It's just not fair!"

Sound familiar? Like a bee in springtime, those same words have stung the heart of every parent. Maybe you're putting emotional compresses over a similar wound, secretly hoping you said the right thing.

But did you? Is everyone on the team really going? Who is and who isn't? How are they getting there? Who will stay with them? How much will it cost? When will they return? With you? With someone else? Most important, how old is your child? Are you giving him or her opportunities to make decisions, and to bear their consequences?

Today's verse of Scripture says that in an abundance of counselors there is victory—for you, and for your child. If a difficult decision faces your family today, perhaps a few phone calls would help. The people you call may see the situation from a different perspective, one that could keep you from a shortsighted or wrong conclusion. Take a moment right now to prayerfully ask the Holy Spirit's direction, then trust His guidance as you seek victory in an abundance of counselors.

PRAYER: Lord, thank You for Your Word. Please lead me to the counselors who can help me make this hard decision about (describe your particular situation). Guide me to the conclusion that will bring honor to You, Father.

The pleasure of gratitude

READ EPHESIANS 5:18-21.
"Always giving thanks for all things in the name of our Lord Jesus Christ to God. . . ."
Ephesians 5:20

Y ou may pick out two cookies—one for now and one for later."

Alesha laughed, bounding from one end of the display case to the other like a cheerleader without pompoms. "I think," she announced at last, "I'll have one of those and one of those." The woman behind the counter placed one sugar and one peanut butter cookie in a bag and gave it to me.

Our grandaughter waited, watching me with large brown eyes until I handed her the sack.

She grinned, peering inside. "Oh thank you, Grandma!"

Her words washed my soul with contentment. I loved this little girl beyond words, and delighted in making her happy. But hearing her say thank you wrapped a ribbon around everything I did for her.

Your heavenly Father longs to hear the same words from you. Think back over the past week. What have you specifically prayed for? How many answers, however small, has He given you? Is your house warm? Can you walk? Did the large-print books for your loved one finally arrive? Does food overflow your shelves and refrigerator? Can you see? Hear?

"Always giving thanks for all things," today's Bible reading reminds us. Cumbersome lists of "if only's" blind most caregivers. Today, ask God to help you recognize at least twenty blessings in your life. Then find a quiet place, and take time to say thank You.

PRAYER: Father, You assure me of Your love in a thousand ways. May I never take Your many blessings for granted.

Peace that passes understanding

———— ✿ ————

READ ISAIAH 26:1-4.
"The steadfast of mind Thou wilt keep in perfect peace." Isaiah 26:3a

Why did I begin every day by rushing to work? I pressed the accelerator, vowing that tonight I would put the alarm across the room before I went to sleep. Too soon I rounded the snow covered bend, glimpsed the state highway 500 feet ahead, and hit the brake.

Like an elephant on ice skates my old station wagon pivoted left as it hurled toward the intersection. I clutched the steering wheel, frozen with fear as the car lurched deeper into its twirl. Suddenly long-frozen instructions thawed in my brain and I jerked my foot off the brake. The lumbering metal dancer shuddered, then completed its turn. Weak with fear, I crept to the roadside twenty feet from the highway, and began to cry.

Sooner or later every caregiving ministry hits black ice. Perhaps your loved one's face turns blue, or he falls out of bed screaming in pain, or gasps for air clutching his chest, or stares up at you, suddenly unable to speak. Without God you will hit the brakes, out of control.

With Him, the Lord promises to keep you in perfect peace. Yes, your hands may turn icy. Yes, your heart may freeze with fear. But despite your feelings He will guide you over the black ice of every future crisis. He will show you exactly what to do, when to do it, and how. He will abundantly supply your needs today, and lead you safely through whatever tomorrow may bring.

PRAYER: Thank You Lord, that Your promises never fail. Keep me in the perfect peace that comes only from You.

Other books by Mary Vaughn Armstrong

- **Caregiving for Your Loved Ones**

- **Golden Gate Morning**